Euripides: *Electra*

COMPANIONS TO GREEK AND ROMAN TRAGEDY

Series Editor: Thomas Harrison

Euripides: *Electra*

Rush Rehm

BLOOMSBURY ACADEMIC
LONDON • NEW YORK • OXFORD • NEW DELHI • SYDNEY

BLOOMSBURY ACADEMIC
Bloomsbury Publishing Plc
50 Bedford Square, London, WC1B 3DP, UK
1385 Broadway, New York, NY 10018, USA
29 Earlsfort Terrace, Dublin 2, Ireland

BLOOMSBURY, BLOOMSBURY ACADEMIC and the Diana logo are trademarks of
Bloomsbury Publishing Plc

First published in Great Britain 2021
This paperback edition published in 2022

A catalogue record for this book is available from the British Library.

Library of Congress Cataloging-in-Publication Data
Names: Rehm, Rush, author. Title: Euripides, Electra / Rush Rehm.
Other titles: Companions to Greek and Roman tragedy. Description: New York : Bloomsbury
Academic, 2020. | Series: Companions to Greek and Roman tragedy | Includes bibliographical
references and index. | Summary: "This new introduction to Euripides' fascinating
interpretation of the story of Electra and her brother Orestes emphasizes its theatricality,
showing how captivating the play remains to this day. Electra poses many challenges for
those drawn to Greek tragedy – students, scholars, actors, directors, stage designers,
readers and audiences. Rush Rehm addresses the most important questions about the play:
its shift in tone between tragedy and humour; why Euripides arranged the plot as he did;
issues of class and gender; the credibility of the gods and heroes, and the power of the
myths that keep their stories alive. A series of concise and engaging chapters explore the
functions of the characters and chorus, and how their roles change over the course of the
play; the language and imagery that affects the audience's response to the events on stage;
the themes at work in the tragedy, and how Euripides forges them into a coherent theatrical
experience; the later reception of the play, and how an array of writers, directors and
filmmakers have interpreted the original. Euripides' Electra has much to say to us in our
contemporary world. This thorough, richly informed introduction challenges our
understanding of what Greek tragedy was and what it can offer modern theatre, perhaps its
most valuable legacy"– Provided by publisher. Identifiers: LCCN 2020023633 (print) |
LCCN 2020023634 (ebook) | ISBN 9781350095670 (hardback) |
ISBN 9781350095687 (ebook) | ISBN 9781350095694 (epub) Subjects: LCSH: Euripides.
Electra. | Greek drama (Tragedy)—History and criticism. Classification: LCC PA3973.E53
R44 2020 (print) | LCC PA3973.E53 (ebook) | DDC 882/.01—dc23
LC record available at https://lccn.loc.gov/2020023633
LC ebook record available at https://lccn.loc.gov/2020023634

ISBN: HB: 978-1-3500-9567-0
        PB: 978-1-3501-9161-7
        ePDF: 978-1-3500-9568-7
        eBook: 978-1-3500-9569-4

Series: Companions to Greek and Roman Tragedy

Typeset by RefineCatch Limited, Bungay, Suffolk

To find out more about our authors and books visit www.bloomsbury.com
and sign up for our newsletters.

Contents

Figures

Introduction

Although conceived with accessibility in mind, this introduction to Euripides' *Electra* assumes that the reader has (at some point) read or seen Euripides' play. If you haven't, let me urge you to do so – you can download my translation (free) at https://stanfordreptheater.com/electratranslation, or consult one of the versions found in References at the end of the book.[1]

Most useful responses to a great play – whether criticism, interpretation, or theatrical production – take us back to the original with renewed interest. If we allow summation, analysis, interpretation, or 'theory' to replace what we're trying to understand, then we've put the cart before the horse. By the logic of the image, this leads to a dead halt, all the more so the higher we pile the cart with things the horse could never pull. Shakespeare's Hamlet says it best: 'The play's the thing'. As you read what follows, keep the play in mind and use it as a touchstone – this is what I have tried to do.

In Chapter 1, I discuss fifth-century Athenian theatre production and the theatrical conventions in which Euripides worked, and which he helped to shape. When possible, I draw on events and passages from *Electra* to illustrate the point in question. In the following seven chapters, I deal more directly with the play itself. Chapter 2 offers a summary of what happens, focusing on its structure and how the story unfolds in performance. Chapter 3 deals with the mythic and dramatic tradition that Euripides' *Electra* drew on and transformed. If we fail to consider the many ways his play reflects (and often rejects) inherited accounts of the myth, we have severely limited our understanding what Euripides accomplishes in his tragedy.

Chapter 4 examines the dramatic characters and some of the challenges they pose for the actors who play them. Acknowledging the power of mythic figures to capture the contemporary imagination, I offer what I hope are helpful insights for those readers drawn to characters more than to plot or to the tragic tradition. In Chapter 5, we shift our focus from the mythic macrocosm to the microcosm of language, style, and poetic imagery. In Greek tragedy, language *matters* in a way that differentiates it from much of our contemporary drama. By attending to the diction of tragic speech, the rhetoric of argument, the imaginative sweep of lyric, and the power of narrative description, we enhance our appreciation of Euripides' play.

Chapter 6 focuses on costumes, props, bodies, and corpses in *Electra*, physical elements that ground dramatic character and language in the materiality of production. The next two chapters deal with important thematic issues in the play. Chapter 7 explores the interrelated themes of gender, sex, children, and childbirth, topics of great interest today as they were in fifth-century BC Athens. Chapter 8 examines the social and economic class differences scrutinized in *Electra*, as well as the complex relationship between earth and sky, and between gods and mortals, subjects of special concern to Euripides. In Chapter 9, we leave ancient Athens and turn our attention to the afterlife of *Electra*, looking at significant productions, adaptations, and transformations of Euripides' play.

I first met Euripides' *Electra* many years ago as an undergraduate learning ancient Greek. I found the play so compelling that I translated and directed it, and over the past several decades I have returned to the play time and again. I am deeply grateful to the series editor Tom Harrison for inviting me to write this Companion, and to the anonymous reader for Bloomsbury Academic, whose close reading and sound advice saved me from several errors. I also thank the American School of Classical Studies, Athens, where I spent several months working on the book, with special appreciation to the ASCSA Director, Professor Jenifer Neils for her kind hospitality; Joëlle Chambon, Associate Maître de conférence, Université Paul-Valéry Montpellier 3, for advice on French versions of *Electra*; the Michael

Cacoyannis Foundation, Athens, Greece, for their generous help with photographs from Cacoyannis's *Elektra*; P.E. Easterling, Regius Professor of Greek (emerita), University of Cambridge, for last-minute email assistance on a textual question when I was marooned (happily, but without a library) on Kythira during the COVID-19 quarantine; and the actors, designers, and production staff with whom I have worked on theatrical productions of *Electra* over the years. It has been a pleasure to engage the thoughts and responses of scholars and theatre artists who have spent time and energy on this challenging, provocative, and quintessentially Euripidean tragedy.[2]

Theatrical Background

To understand an ancient play like *Electra*, we need to know what we can about the theatrical environment that brought it into being. Following the establishment of democracy in 508–507 BC, the city of Athens celebrated theatrical performances at the City Dionysia, a weeklong festival dedicated to the god Dionysus. Held each spring in the open-air theatre on the south slope of the Acropolis (site of the famous Parthenon), the performances attracted large crowds and were open to all who could afford a ticket.[1] The festival featured competitions in tragedy (three playwrights entered three tragedies and a satyr-play each), comedy (five playwrights entered one play each), and dithyramb (ten adult male choruses and ten boys' choruses sang and danced narrative poems dedicated to Dionysus).[2] Sometime between 422 and 413 BC, Euripides' *Electra* premiered at the City Dionysia. Although the titles of the two other tragedies and the satyr play Euripides entered that year are unknown, seventeen additional plays of his survive, as well as the names of many more.[3]

Shielded from the north wind, the theatre of Dionysus took its shape from the curve of the hillside that formed a natural *theatron*, 'a place for seeing'. From where the audience gathered, a panorama opened up over the southern part of the city of Athens, with Mt. Hymettus and the Ilissos river to the east, the city and lowlands leading down to the Bay of Phaleron to the south (with the peaked island of Aegina rising in the distance in the Saronic Gulf), and the Hill of the Muses and the Pnyx (where the Athenian Assembly met) to the west – all visible from various points in the theatre.

As well as providing distant vistas, the theatre of Dionysus drew the audience's attention to the performance area, called the *orchêstra*. This

Fig. 1 Theatre of Dionysus in Athens, late nineteenth century. Courtesy of Deutsches Archäologisches Institut-Athen.

flattened surface of beaten earth followed the contours of the slope where the audience sat, bounded by the retaining wall built behind and just below the *orchêstra* to keep it from eroding down the hillside.[4] Although a few stone seating blocks from the fifth century have come to light, we know from the comic playwright Aristophanes that some audience members sat on wooden benches. Archaeologists recently have found indications that scaffolding for seats was erected for the festival and removed afterwards. The rest of the audience sat (or stood) on the hillside rising above the temporary seating banks. Even in Euripides' day, the theatre of Dionysus had a makeshift quality to it.

The same applies to the *skênê* façade, a temporary wooden structure that represented the play's setting – a temple, a palace, or in the case of *Electra* a poor farmer's cottage in the country. A central opening in the façade allowed actors to enter and exit the playing area, providing access to the stage building behind the *orchêstra*, where the actors could change masks and costumes without being seen. When a playwright wished to reveal the body of someone (usually dead) inside, the doorway opened and a wheeled cart (*ekkuklêma*) rolled out with the corpse on it. Near the end of *Electra*, Euripides turns the Farmer's cottage 'inside out' by using the *ekkuklêma* to reveal the corpses of Clytemnestra and Aegisthus.[5]

The stage building also could support actors on its roof, an area known as the *theologeion* ('place where the gods speak') because stage divinities often appeared there. At the end of *Electra*, Castor and Polydeuces (the semi-divine brothers of Clytemnestra and Helen) arrive on the roof by means of the *mêchanê* ('machine'), from whence we get the Latin phrase *deus ex machina*, 'god from the machine'. A lever-and-fulcrum apparatus located behind the *skênê* raised the actors above the roof and then lowered them onto it, where they spoke from 'on high'.[6] Euripides' Chorus convey their amazement, even incredulity, at the twin gods' arrival: 'But look, high, high above the house / some mighty spirits or heavenly gods / are coming our way. This is not the path / that humans walk. Why do they appear / so plainly to our mortal eyes?' (Eur. *El.* 1233–37).

Human characters who came from far away normally arrived and departed through one of the two *parodoi* ('side roads', also called *eisodoi*, 'roads in'), formed by the gap between the ends of the *skênê* façade and the front row of seats. Choruses almost always made their initial entrance through one of the *parodoi* (giving their entry song the name *parodos*), indicating that they – like the Chorus of *Electra* – had to travel some distance to reach the location where the play is set. These side entrances were wide enough to allow horse-drawn carts to drive into the *orchêstra*, as Clytemnestra does (accompanied by her Trojan slaves) when she visits Electra's cottage.

Because the audience could see a character approaching from the distance, either that character or someone onstage would announce the arrival with lines that 'covered' the entrance. This helps account for the Old Man's self-description as he makes his way into the *orchêstra* through an *eisodos*:

> Where, where is the young princess, my dear mistress
> and child of Agamemnon, whom I reared so long ago?
> What a steep approach she has to her house, difficult for this tired,
> bent old man to walk up, putting one foot in front of the other.
> Still, for the sake of my friends I must drag myself along,
> stooped over, weak-kneed, wavering, but still walking.
>   Oh daughter, now I see you coming from the house ...
>
> *El.* 487–93

During his long entrance, the Old Man provides the audience with important information: decades before, he raised the young Agamemnon; he knows Agamemnon's daughter Electra well; her cottage lies on a steep hill, hard to reach for someone old and frail like himself; he remains devoted to the family, in spite of the effort it costs him.

The size of the open-air theatre, the public nature of the festival, and the scale of the tragic myths help account for conventions of ancient Greek performance. To provide some perspective, actors and audiences in fifth-century Athens would not have known what to make of Ibsen's *Hedda Gabler*. Written for an actress in the title role, the play imagines an audience that looked through the 'fourth wall' into a private room, where characters used everyday conversation and behaviour to reveal (or hide) the truth of their inner lives. By contrast, Euripides wrote for male performers (both actors and Chorus members), all of whom wore masks that fully covered their face and hair.[7] How could a masked male performer credibly portray a complex heroine like Electra? How could he bring her character to life, if the spectators could not see his facial expressions, the glint in his eye, the smile and snarl of his mouth, his flaring nostrils and furrowed brows?

Far from hindering the tragic actor, the mask helped project his character-persona out to a large audience. Familiarity with the text, facility with language, control over rhythm and inflection, vocal projection, mastery of movement and gesture mattered more for the actor than 'identification' with the imaginary inner life of the character he was playing. To be sure, tragedy seethes with emotions, but in the ancient theatre these feelings were 'externalized'. Whatever an actor wished to convey needed to find a scale that matched the theatre and the 'larger than life' nature of the dramatized myths.[8] Tragedians composed their plays with these criteria in mind.

At the opening of *Electra*, the Farmer comes out of his cottage to give the background of the story (*El.* 1–53).[9] With no one else onstage, to whom is the Farmer speaking? If he were voicing aloud his private thoughts, would he continue talking for fifty lines without interruption? Orestes delivers what amounts to a second prologue (*El.* 82–106), explaining his cautious return from exile. He cannot be sharing the information for the benefit of his companion Pylades; the pair has been travelling together for days.

We need to understand that 'Greek drama was not simply played before an audience (whose existence is tacitly ignored in modern realistic drama), but *to* an audience which was directly addressed so often that its presence was taken for granted by the actors throughout the performance'.[10] All the speeches in *Electra* demand an outward, front-footed, audience-orientated acting style, in which the truth (or what passes for it) depends on its public disclosure. This applies to long speeches like the two prologues, and also to dialogue between two characters, which often takes the form of rapid alternating lines called *stichomythia*. Unspoken feelings, *sotto voce* asides, and muted inner monologues would have made no impact on an audience at the theatre of Dionysus.[11]

By enabling the performer to play different ages and genders, masks help explain the so-called 'three-actor rule' that operated at the City Dionysia. The city of Athens provided each playwright with three actors who performed all the (non-choral) speaking roles, and in 449 BC the festival instituted a prize for the best actor. In *Electra*, the protagonist ('first competitor') played Electra, the second actor played Orestes, and the third actor took on the remaining roles – the Farmer, the old Tutor, the Messenger, Clytemnestra, and Castor – changing his mask, costume, vocal register, and physical demeanour with speed and dexterity.[12]

A tragic convention even more challenging for modern audiences is the Chorus. Like all Greek tragedies, *Electra* alternates scenes of spoken verse with lyric sections sung and danced by a fifteen-member ensemble.[13] In Euripides' play, this group represents girlfriends of Electra who come to invite her to a festival in Argos. Their motivation quickly drops away, however, for the Chorus performs a far more important function. Combining movement, music, and sung (or chanted) poetry, they gather various mythic strands of the story, singing of the Trojan War, the shield of Achilles, the murder of Agamemnon, and the changing fortunes of the house of Atreus. The Chorus recreate significant events that at first may seem disconnected from the plot (the Greek armada crossing the Aegean, the golden lamb brought to the palace in Argos), but that ultimately serve the drama. Affecting the mood in the theatre, the Chorus close off one event, prepare for the next, and open up the play in unexpected ways. As we see in *Electra*, their choral lyric moves freely over space and time, not bound to the constraints of the Chorus's character or the demands of the plot.

Chorus in Greek means 'dance'; our word 'choreography' literally means 'dance writing'. Tragic playwrights did just that, for they not only wrote and staged their plays, but they also came up with the movement for the Chorus and composed the music that accompanied it. The Greek term for 'directing a play' – *didaskein choron* – translates 'to teach a chorus', indicating the importance of the ensemble and their lyric mode in tragedy. After their initial entry (the *parodos*), the Chorus remain onstage for the duration of the play, providing continuity while the other characters come and go.[14] Once established in the *orchêstra*, they perform odes called *stasima* ('standing songs'), lyric passages of great poetic and rhythmic variety. Positioned near the Chorus, a solo musician called an *aulêtês* ('player of the *aulos*', a reed instrument somewhat like a clarinet) accompanied the choral performance.[15]

The metres of tragic lyric can be extremely complicated, all the more so because the rhythmic pattern in one stanza (called a *strophê* or 'turn') is often repeated exactly in the next (*antistrophê*, 'counter-turn'). Classicists call this lyric structure 'responsion', because one stanza 'responds' exactly to another. The playwright can then introduce a new metrical pattern in the third stanza (a second *strophê*), closely matched in its corresponding fourth stanza (second *antistrophê*). Euripides follows this basic choral structure in *Electra*, although the Chorus end their first *stasimon* with a fifth 'stand-alone' stanza (without responsion), called an *epode* ('after song'). In addition to these full-fledged lyrics, the Chorus sing a brief interlude (without responsion) following the reunion of Orestes and Electra, and they introduce the unexpected arrival of Castor and Polydeuces with a short passage of anapests, a metre closer to normal speech than most lyric.

Sometimes a character in tragedy will adopt the lyric mode, performing a 'monody' or 'solo song'. Famous in antiquity for his use of singing actors, Euripides has Electra sing just such a monody when she returns from the spring (*El.* 112–66). Urging herself to keep moving, she laments her brother's exile and her father's murder: 'Hurry, time is ripe, rouse your step – oh gods! / Walk on, walk on, but always weeping, / me, me alone' (*El.* 112–14, repeated at 127–29). After they kill Clytemnestra, Electra and Orestes join the Chorus in a shared lyric called a *kommos*, the Greek term for 'beating ones breast in mourning', associated with funeral lament. By adopting the choral mode, the forlorn brother and sister express in a more musical way their horror at what they have done, and what it means for their future.

For all his theatrical ingenuity, Euripides (480–406 BC) met stiff competition at the City Dionysia. The great tragedian Aeschylus (525–456 BC) died the year before Euripides made his premiere at the festival, but Sophocles (496–405 BC) already had established himself as a formidable rival. His plays (roughly 123 in all, including an *Electra*) won about half the time he competed at the City Dionysia, eighteen victories over Sophocles' long career. This compares with five victories for Euripides, including his posthumous prize in 405 BC for *Bacchae*, *Iphigenia in Aulis*, and *Alcmaeon in Corinth*, probably staged by his son (or nephew) Euripides the Younger, also a tragic playwright.[16]

In spite of Euripides' relatively few first prizes, the fact that the city consistently produced his plays testifies to his continued popularity over a span of five decades. Aristophanes exploits this fact in his comedy *The Frogs*, staged in 404 BC. In a contest in the underworld organized by Dionysus (the god of theatre, played as a comic character), the newly deceased Euripides competes with the long-dead Aeschylus for the honour of returning to Athens to save the city with a performance of one of his tragedies. Although Euripides pulls out all the stops, Dionysus chooses Aeschylus. As he leaves for Athens, Aeschylus hands over his poetic 'chair' in Hades to Sophocles, insisting that Euripides never gets to sit there, even by accident.

Two years before his death in 456 BC, Aeschylus presented his *Oresteia* at the City Dionysia, and the 22-year-old Euripides may well have been in the audience. In his dramatization of the fortunes of the house of Atreus, Aeschylus tells roughly the same story that Euripides tells forty years later in his *Electra*, and that Sophocles also presents in his tragedy of the same name. Aeschylus's trilogy covers Agamemnon's homecoming from Troy and murder by his wife Clytemnestra; the subsequent return of their exiled son Orestes, who reunites with his sister Electra and takes revenge on his mother and her husband Aegisthus; and the suffering that Orestes endures as a matricide, until a trial in Athens sets him free.

Sophocles and Euripides re-worked Aeschylus's version of the story, focusing on Orestes' sister Electra and her role in keeping the flame burning until Orestes can exact vengeance for his father's murder. In his *Electra*, Euripides refers explicitly to passages in the *Oresteia*, exposing what might seem like Aeschylean incompetence to serve his own dramatic ends. We will discuss the relationship of these three versions further in Chapter 3, where we also address the relative dates of Euripides' and Sophocles' *Electra*'s.

The tragedians drew on many earlier sources for myths connected to the house of Atreus, but none were more important than the *Iliad* and *Odyssey*, the Homeric epics that deal with the Trojan War and its aftermath. At the great Panathenaia (the festival procession is represented on the Parthenon frieze), Athenians attended public recitations of these poems by rhapsodes who competed for prizes. These 'stitchers of song' (the literal meaning of 'rhapsodes') resembled tragic actors, for more than half the lines they recited quote the direct speech of characters in Homer's poems – Achilles, Agamemnon, Odysseus, Ajax, Menelaus, Helen, Hector, Hecuba, Andromache, Cassandra, Philoctetes, all of whom reappear in Greek tragedy.

The Homeric poems also include extended narrative passages, which seem to have influenced another convention of Greek tragedy, the Messenger speech. An unnamed character, often only tangentially connected to the action, narrates an offstage event that usually involves violent death. To establish credibility and enhance the impact on the audience, the Messenger quotes the direct speech of those on the scene, verbally recreating the 'mini play' he witnessed offstage. Recounting the murder of Aegisthus in *Electra*, for example, the Messenger describes the setting of Aegisthus's feast, the arrival of the newcomers, the sacrifice that precedes the banquet, Orestes' murder of Aegisthus, and his recognition by loyal palace retainers. In laying out what transpired, the Messenger quotes Aegisthus and Orestes a total of seven times, a technique examined further in Chapter 4.

Euripides developed the possibilities of the Messenger speech with a passion: the horrific immolation of Creusa and Creon in *Medea*, the gut-wrenching dismemberment of Pentheus in *Bacchae*, the brutal smashing of Aegisthus's backbone in *Electra*. Descriptions such as these stood out so vividly that they inspired Greek vase painters, who depicted the scenes as if they actually had taken place onstage.[17] Vase painters did what ancient audiences were encouraged to do: allow the words of the Messenger to spark their imagination until they visualized the offstage events for themselves. We might contrast this process with our current addiction to cinematic overkill, with rivers of (fake) blood, chain-sawed limbs, and special effects that overwhelm the spectators rather than engage their imaginations. We return to this issue in the final chapter.

In Sophocles' *Electra*, the Messenger exploits the power of verbal description in a new way, for the purposes of deception. Agamemnon's old Tutor (in disguise) spins out a riveting account of Orestes' supposed death in a chariot race at the Pythian games in Delphi, a fabrication designed to gain Orestes access to the palace. Aware of the deceit, the audience watch the contrasting reactions of Clytemnestra and Electra to the news. The tripartite audience of his speech – the crowd at the imaginary games, the dramatic characters and Chorus onstage, and the spectators in the theatre – experience the excitement of athletic competition, even as they respond to Orestes' 'death' in different ways.

Athletic events in ancient Greece attracted large crowds and produced celebrity victors, for whom choral performances of *epinician* odes ('songs after victory') were commissioned, especially at great Panhellenic games. This performance genre finds its way into Euripides' *Electra*. Orestes and Pylades pretend to be athletes on their way to the Olympic games, and the unsuspecting Aegisthus invites them to join his sacrifice and feast. After Orestes murders Aegisthus, the Chorus sing a short lyric that praises him, modelled on an *epinician* ode (*El.* 860–65, 874–79). Electra then crowns her brother and Pylades for winning a far greater contest than a sporting event, analysed further in Chapter 5.

Music and choral performances occurred in other celebratory contexts in ancient Greece, including festivals and weddings. The Chorus invite Electra to join them at the festival for new brides and unwed maidens, who will dance before the temple of Hera, the goddess of marriage. Ashamed of her liminal status, Electra prefers 'not to take my place in a chorus / with Argive brides, my whirling feet / striking the ground' (*El.* 178–80).[18] Time and again Electra laments the wedding she never had, having been forced into a union with the Farmer, one that remains unconsummated. After her mother's murder, the bloodstained Electra thinks again about the wedding ritual that has eluded her: 'Ah, me, me. Where can I go? What choral dance? / What marriage? What husband would lead me / to a bridal bed? (*El.* 1198–1200). Denied a proper nuptial ceremony, with its music, dance, and public festivity, Electra feels deprived of a full life.

As noted above, an *aulos* player accompanied tragedy, comedy, dithyramb, and other choral performances. The instrument also set the rhythm for military marches and for the rowers in the Athenian navy.[19] In *Electra*, the Chorus imagine the naval expedition to Troy as a kind of dance, the Greek ships escorted by 'a chorus (*choreumata*) of Nereids [sea nymphs] / and *aulos*-loving dolphins / that moved in consort / with the dark blue prows' (*El.* 434–37). In a self-reflexive gesture analysed further in Chapter 4, Electra's friends perform a lyric chorus in which the scene they describe resembles their own performance onstage.

In addition to theatre, athletic games, wedding rituals, and festival choruses, public events of a different sort helped distinguish Athens from other Greek cities. The democratic Assembly and the people's law courts placed a premium on public speaking and mastery of verbal strategies that could move an audience. Not surprisingly, tragedians drew on these political and judicial practices, and their plays bristle with rhetorical tropes, legal language, argumentative exchanges, and trial-like scenarios. Euripides often pairs speakers making contradictory cases, like a plaintiff and defendant at a trial, or a debate between opposing parties in the Assembly. The confrontation between Electra and Clytemnestra follows this pattern, a balanced exchange in which each delivers a speech of thirty-nine lines, reflecting the equal time-allotments for speeches at jury trials in Athens (*El.* 1011–50, 1060–99).[20]

In the Athenian law courts, professional speechwriters usually wrote the words delivered by the plaintiffs and defendants, turning litigants into quasi-performers acting out a scripted role. Greek tragedians found role-playing an endless fascination, and tragic characters frequently use deceit, deception, and even false identities to further their plans. In *Electra*, Euripides has Orestes arrive incognito to the Argive countryside, where he hides his identity from his sister (Sophocles uses the same strategy in his *Electra*). Only the relentless inquisitiveness of the old Tutor forces Orestes to drop his disguise and admit who he is. When invited to Aegisthus's feast, Orestes and Pylades claim to be Thessalians headed for the Olympic games, a subterfuge that leads to Aegisthus's murder. The most disturbing deception of all involves Electra's claim that she has just given birth to a son, a fiction that lures her mother from the palace to the countryside. When she enters the cottage, instead of a new-born grandchild Clytemnestra finds her grown-up son, who cuts her down with the help of his sister.

From wedding ritual to the law courts, from epic recitations to victory odes, from athletic competitions to political debates, performance played an essential role in the Athens of Euripides' day. The various performance elements found their way into tragedy, merging ancient myth with contemporary practice and grounding the plays in a recognizable fifth-century context. The engaging power of this double vision – mythic tradition and the 'now' of the audience – made tragic performances like that of *Electra* a touchstone for Athenian society.

What Happens and How

In his *Poetics*, Aristotle famously considers 'plot' (*muthos*) as 'the soul (*psychê*, "animating principle") of tragedy',[1] meaning that the shaping of events takes precedence over the characters who get caught up in them. Whether one agrees with Aristotle or not, a solid grasp of the dramatic architecture of *Electra* will allow us to understand better how Euripides re-works elements of the myth found in earlier versions (Chapter 3), and to appreciate the interaction of characters with one another (Chapter 4), the power of language and imagery (Chapter 5), and important themes and their development (Chapters 6 through 8).

When discussing tragic structure, scholars tend to apply generic categories across Greek tragedy, using terms like 'prologue' (everything that takes place before the first choral ode), *parodos* (the first choral ode, usually an entry song), *epeisodion* ('episode' or 'act', what takes place between each choral ode), *stasimon* ('standing chorus', sometimes called an 'act-dividing' song), and *exodos* (everything that happens after the final choral *stasimon*).

While using these terms when helpful, I offer a more theatrical approach to the plot of *Electra*, the way a stage director might break down the play into manageable sections for rehearsal. Important issues include who enters, who else is onstage, what expressive mode they employ (spoken or lyric metres, the latter accompanied by the *aulos*), what happens between or among them, when they depart, where they go, and how what has transpired feeds into what happens next. As playwright and director, Euripides addressed these questions when he prepared his tragedy for the City Dionysia.

The following outline lays out five broad 'movements' in *Electra*,[2] each separated by a significant arrival or departure, a shift from dialogue into speech, or a change from speech into lyric. Within each movement, I identify the sequence of important events, listing line numbers and speakers (I leave out the Chorus leader when delivering short interstitial passages).[3] Characters in brackets are present but do not speak; after their entrance in the *parodos*, the Chorus remain onstage throughout. To clarify the basic action or focus of each section, I give short titles to each one, following the German playwright Bertolt Brecht's method in his *Lehrstücke* ('learning plays').[4] By suggesting a name for each section (you can come up with your own), one can better understand why Euripides builds *Electra* the way he does, and how these smaller units cohere into the tragedy as a whole.

First movement (1–431)

1. *The set up* (1–81)
    (a) *Myth and marriage* (Farmer 1–53)
As noted in Chapter 1, Euripides begins most of his tragedies with a prologue, in which a character explains the background to the story. *Electra* needs such an introduction, because Euripides changes several key elements in the myth – most importantly, he moves the location from the palace in Argos to a cottage in the Argive hills, and he has Electra 'married off' to the Farmer who lives there.

Summarizing significant events from the past, the Farmer contrasts Agamemnon's victory as the Greek commander at Troy with his disastrous homecoming, killed by his wife Clytemnestra and her lover Aegisthus. After seizing power, Aegisthus drove Agamemnon's son Orestes into exile with a price on his head, and then he married Orestes' sister Electra to the Farmer. Because of his low social and economic status, the Farmer cannot father claimants to the throne, but he has no desire to take advantage of his wife, and Electra remains a virgin. The Farmer insists that this will prove the wiser course in the end.

    (b) *Black night* (Electra 54–63)
Without noticing her husband, Electra enters from the cottage with a jug to fetch water. Addressing the night sky, she laments her father's death, admitting that she goes to the nearby spring not because she has

to, but to show the gods how Aegisthus has destroyed her life. Her mother Clytemnestra bears his children, threatening Electra and Orestes' rightful claim to the palace. Electra's reference to the night and the Farmer's mention of daybreak (line 79) indicate that they are both caught up in the working rhythms of farm life.[5]

(c) *Collaboration* (Electra, Farmer 64–76)

Making his presence known, the Farmer offers to get the water for his wife, having told her before not to demean herself on his account. Electra insists that she performs these chores happily to lighten her husband's burdens, and she exits with her jug out of the theatre. Although most editors think Electra exits with the Farmer at line 81, it makes more sense to end the scene as it began, with the Farmer alone onstage, a pattern repeated with the Farmer's final exit from the play (line 431).

(d) *Work, not prayers* (Farmer 77–81)

Noting that the spring does not lie far from the house, the Farmer ends the scene with what sounds like a folk saying: 'Work, not prayers, puts food on the table'. He leaves to begin the spring ploughing and sowing, using the same *eisodos* from which Electra exited a few lines before.

2. *Cautious return* (Orestes [Pylades; two servants] 82–111)

Orestes, Pylades, and servants enter the now-empty *orchêstra* through the opposite *eisodos*.[6] In what amounts to a second prologue, Orestes explains his furtive return to the Argive border, fearing Aegisthus, whom he has come to kill. After consulting Apollo's oracle at Delphi, Orestes offered sacrifice at his father's tomb, located far from the palace. He has heard that his sister is married, and here in the countryside he hopes to learn more about what has happened. When Electra returns from the spring, Orestes mistakes her for a slave woman, and he and his men hide to find out what they can, without being found out themselves.

3. *Waters of grief* (Electra 112–66)

Carrying the pitcher filled with fresh water on her head, Electra enters through the same *eisodos* from which she left. She performs a solo lyric (monody), in which she laments her life as child of Agamemnon and Clytemnestra. She cannot forget her father's fate, murdered in the bath by her mother, and she longs to take revenge or die. The audience knows that Orestes watches in hiding, now fully aware that the farmwoman is his sister Electra.

4. *The (non) festival* (Chorus, Electra 167–219)

Unexpectedly, a Chorus of excited young women arrive through a side entrance. They have come to invite Electra to a festival honouring Hera, goddess of brides and marriage.[7] Having just finished her monody, Electra responds in lyric, in effect joining the Chorus's entry song. Lacking clothes and adornments befitting a princess, she tells them that festivals and dances hold no interest for her, and she rejects their offer to loan her their robes and jewellery. She repeats a litany of grief for her father, for Orestes, and for her own impoverished life.

Moving into dialogue meter, the Chorus leader expresses their sympathy.[8] Suddenly Electra sees men in hiding whom she takes for criminals, and she tells the Chorus to flee. By shifting from lyric into the normal metre for speech, Euripides signals the return to what we assume is the business at hand: the impending reunion of Orestes and Electra. No one in the play mentions the festival of Hera again.

Fig. 2 Elektra (Lydia Koniordou) and Chorus, from *Elektra* (1989), directed by Kostas Tsianos, Municipal Regional Theatre of Larissa, Thessaliko Theatro. Courtesy of Thessaliko Theatro.

5. *First encounters* (Orestes, Electra, Farmer [Chorus, Pylades, servants] 220–338)

(a) *Keep your distance* (Orestes, Electra 220–89)

Initiating a dialogue of alternating single lines (*stichomythia*, or 'line-speech'), Orestes allays Electra's fears by claiming he brings news from her brother. Tragedians often use *stichomythia* to forge a link between two characters that leads to concerted action. Here, however, the exchange dramatizes a failed connection, for it does not deliver the recognition that we would expect.[9] Orestes learns of Electra's 'death-like marriage' (247), and also of his sister's virginity, which he attributes to the Farmer's fear of her brother's return. Electra corrects him: her husband respects her and her lineage (257–61). Assuring the stranger of the Chorus's loyalty, Electra boasts of her readiness to kill her mother 'with the same axe that took my father's life' (279). She wonders at Orestes' long absence and admits that she would not know him if she saw him. Only the old Tutor of Agamemnon, who helped Orestes escape into exile, could recognize her brother now.

(b) *Say more* (Orestes, Chorus 290–99)

Following the long stichomythic exchange, Orestes and the Chorus ask Electra to elaborate her hardships. The Chorus leader's lines (bland and repetitive) mark the transition to a new speaker and to a different expressive mode, shifting from dialogue to the monologue (uninterrupted speech) of Electra.

(c) *My wretched life* (Electra 300–38)

Electra describes her forced marriage, poverty, endless labour, and ragged clothes, a life 'deprived of festivals and choral dance' (310). She contrasts her impoverished existence with her mother's luxurious life in the palace, and she recounts the crass excesses of Aegisthus. Lording it over the city, he brandishes the royal sceptre in his bloodstained hands; drunk, he abuses Agamemnon's grave and hurls taunts at the long-absent Orestes. Electra begs the stranger to report all this to her brother, whose failure to return and take revenge disgraces his father's name and legacy. For all its lively detail, Electra's speech represents the third time the audience has heard her litany of woe; Orestes heard the second instalment while in hiding.[10]

6. *Hospitality* (Farmer, Electra, Orestes [Chorus, Pylades, servants]
   339–431)

(a) *Open house* (Farmer, Electra 339–63)

Announced by the Chorus, the Farmer returns from his fields, shocked
at the sight of his wife talking to strange men. Once he learns that these
strangers bring news of Orestes, the Farmer changes his tune, opening
his doors with effusive generosity. Most commentators think that the
Farmer remains onstage during Orestes' long speech. But it makes
more sense for the Farmer to enter the cottage after his welcome (363)
as if to make things ready, and then return to the stage near the end of
Orestes' reflections, prompting the young man to accept the invitation
and go into the cottage.

(b) *Fallen signposts* (Orestes 364–90)

Having met Electra's husband (364–66), Orestes works through this
conundrum: how can such nobility spring from a poor farmer? He
considers the gap between appearance and reality: what external signs
should we focus on, and how should we read them, to arrive at the
truth? How can we differentiate inherited privilege from true nobility?
These questions resonate throughout the play; here, they deliver an
implicit judgement on the speaker, for Orestes seems oblivious to what
his conclusions might say about himself.

(c) *In we go* (Orestes 391–400; also Pylades and servants enter the
   cottage)

Concluding his reflection, Orestes finally accepts the invitation to enter
the house: 'Well, since we are your worthy guests / . . . / let us accept
what hospitality there is' (391–93). His insistence that his entourage
must go in (393–94) suggests that the prospect has limited appeal. As
we shall see, Orestes' entrance marks the beginning of a major shift in
the play, the gradual transformation of the Farmer's cottage into a
makeshift house of Atreus, more appropriate for deceit, betrayal, and
bloodshed than for fresh water brought back from the spring.

(d) *How could you?* (Electra, Farmer 401–25)

The Chorus leader delivers a few lines to cover the exit of Orestes and
his entourage, signalling the start of a new dialogue. Deaf to Orestes'
praise of the Farmer's generosity, Electra rails at her husband as a
'thoughtless fool' (404) for inviting such noble visitors into their poor
dwelling. She commands him to go find the old Tutor of her father,

now a shepherd in the country, and ask him to bring proper provisions for the guests. Agreeing to fetch the old man, the Farmer tells Electra to go inside and prepare something, a task he insists she can manage.

(e) *Last thoughts* (Farmer 426–31)

Following Electra's exit into the cottage, the Farmer remains onstage, as was probably the case after Electra left to fetch water earlier (line 77). The Farmer's coda on the value (and limits) of wealth marks the last we hear from him. After his exit, the actor soon returns as the Old Man, tutor of Agamemnon, who moves the play towards recognition and revenge.

Second movement (432–698)

7. *The armour of Achilles* (Chorus 432–86)

In their first *stasimon*, the Chorus begin the transition from the relative innocence of the opening movement to the bloodshed that lies ahead. Going back one generation, they imagine an idyllic scene of the Greek ships sailing off to the Trojan War, accompanied by a joyful dance of Nereids (sea-nymphs) and *aulos*-loving dolphins (*strophê* 'a', 432–41). They then move further back in time, before the armada (*antistrophê* 'a', 442–51), singing of the Nereids who brought armour to the Greek hero Achilles in the uplands of Mt. Pelion, where the young man received his education from the centaur Chiron.

The Chorus' tone darkens in the second stanza, when they recount the myths illustrated on the armour.[11] The stories etched into the shield fill the Trojans with terror, especially the image of Perseus holding the severed head of the gorgon, whose gaze could turn a man to stone (*strophê* 'b', 452–63). Achilles' helmet shows sphinxes tearing apart their victims, and the breastplate depicts Bellerophon's battle against the monstrous Chimaera (*antistrophê* 'b', 464–75).

In the epode (476–86), the Chorus describe Achilles' sword, its handle engraved with galloping horses that seem to raise black dust from the metal surface. The young women abruptly shift their focus to the adulterous Clytemnestra, who killed Agamemnon, the leader of the Greeks at Troy. One day they hope to see her neck dripping with gore, as if the sword of Achilles had been forged to slit her throat. Forsaking the lyrical tone of the opening section, the Chorus end the first *stasimon* with violence and bloodshed.

8. *Signs of Orestes* (Old Man, Electra [Chorus] 487–548)

Complaining of the steep approach, the Old Man enters through an *eisodos*, bringing supplies to welcome Electra's guests. In spite of the occasion, he has been weeping, and he dries his tears on his tattered clothes. On the way he paid a visit to the grave of Agamemnon to pour a libation in his honour. There he noticed that someone else had sacrificed a black lamb and left a lock of hair at the tomb. Convinced that the offerings came from Orestes, he asks Electra to compare the lock of hair to her own, an idea she ridicules.[12] The Old Man then tells her to compare her footprints with those left by the visitor at the gravesite. Electra rejects this idea as equally absurd, along with the Old Man's suggestion that the cloth she wove for the young Orestes might help her recognize her brother. Electra doubts the Old Man's sanity, but he remains undeterred and wants to take stock of the strangers.

9. *Who am I?* (Old Man, Electra, Orestes [Pylades, servants, Chorus] 549–84)

The drive towards the recognition moves into high gear with the entrance of Orestes, Pylades, and servants from the cottage. Orestes wonders who this 'ancient relic' (554) might be, and Electra informs him that the Old Man was once Agamemnon's Tutor, who saved Orestes from Aegisthus. Inspecting the stranger at close range, the Old Man announces to the incredulous Electra that he is Orestes. The scar over her brother's eye, the sign of a childhood fall, proves it. A swift eight-line recognition follows, including three lines of shared *stichomythia* between Orestes and Electra, each speaking half a line each. This rapid-fire dialogue brings to fulfilment their earlier stichomythic exchange (lines 230–89), which failed to lead to recognition. Reunited at last, the siblings embrace.[13]

10. *You have come!* (Chorus 585–95)

A brief choral celebration (a single stanza) helps effect the transition from recognition to revenge. Comparing Orestes to a torch that dispels the darkness, the Chorus praise the gods for bringing Electra's brother home, signalling victory for his father's house.[14]

11. *Planning revenge* (Orestes, Old Man, Electra [Pylades, servants, Chorus] 596–698)

Releasing his embrace of Electra, Orestes poses a series of questions to the Old Man: How can I take revenge? Will anyone in Argos help? Am I bankrupt in friends as well as fortune? What path should I take against my enemies? In the *stichomythia* that follows, the Old Man guides Orestes towards vengeance. Knowing that Aegisthus is offering sacrifice to the Nymphs in the fields, the Old Man instructs Orestes on how he might confront his mortal enemy without having to risk entry into the palace.

When Orestes asks how he can kill Clytemnestra, who did not accompany her husband, Electra suddenly speaks after sixty lines of silence: 'I myself will handle the murder of my mother' (647). Replacing Orestes in the stichomythic exchange, she tells the Old Man to bring the (false) news to Clytemnestra that her daughter has given birth to a son.[15] When the queen comes to the cottage to help with the postpartum ritual and 'mourn the low status of my child' (658), Electra will kill her.

Brother and sister pray for help, calling on Zeus (the father of their mythic ancestor Tantalus), on Hera (patron goddess of Argos), on their murdered father Agamemnon, and on the Earth (who will gather the spirits of the Greeks who died at Troy). Encouraging her brother in his fight against Aegisthus, Electra tells the Chorus to report news of the outcome 'with beacon clarity' (694). If Orestes fails, she vows to kill herself to keep her enemies from 'raping my body' (698). Orestes, Pylades, the servants, and the Old Man exit via an *eisodos*; Electra enters the cottage.

Third movement (699–961)

12. Myth of the golden lamb (Chorus 699–746)
Left alone in the *orchêstra*, the Chorus perform the second *stasimon*. Similar to the previous ode, they turn to a mythic subject, this time from the generation before the Trojan War. The Chorus sing of a magical golden lamb that Pan endowed with regal significance for the house of Atreus (699–712). Thyestes seduced his brother Atreus's wife Aerope, stole the lamb, and seized political power (713–26). In the second *strophê*, the Chorus describe the gods' reaction to the lamb's theft, when an angry Zeus reversed the path of the stars and the sun

(which formerly had moved west to east across the sky), bringing rain to the northern lands and parching the south (727–36).

In the *antistrophê* (737–46), the Chorus question the myth they have just invoked, doubting that the gods care enough about mortal folly to unleash such a cosmic upheaval. They conclude that, although untrue, such tales encourage humans to behave morally out of fear for the repercussions. As in the previous *stasimon*, the Chorus end their lyric by suddenly shifting focus, condemning Clytemnestra for murdering her husband (745–46).

13. *Where is the Messenger?* (Chorus, Electra, Messenger 747–73)
Shouts heard in the distance prompt the Chorus to call Electra from the cottage. Fearing the worst, she threatens to kill herself. 'Where are the messengers?' she cries (759), referring to the convention of the messenger speech discussed in Chapter 1. The Messenger arrives two lines later with news of Orestes' victory, but Electra fails to recognize him: 'How can I trust what you report?' (765). In no other Greek tragedy does a character question a Messenger's arrival or reliability.[16] Orestes' servant quickly establishes his identity and reports his master's triumph over Aegisthus.

14. *Aegisthus's murder* (Messenger [Electra, Chorus] 774–858)
In the longest speech in the play, the Messenger tells how Orestes and Pylades gained Aegisthus's confidence and killed him. Claiming to be Thessalians on their way to the sanctuary of Zeus at Olympia, they accept Aegisthus's invitation to join his sacrifice and feast. The Messenger describes the ritual preparations: the purifying lustrations (which Orestes and Pylades avoid, claiming they had just washed in the flowing river), the bowl to catch the victim's blood, the baskets with barley to sprinkle on the altar, the blazing fire and cauldrons, the sacrificial knife.

Praying that his enemies suffer, Aegisthus dedicates a lock of the bullock's hair on the altar and slits the animal's throat. He asks the stranger to flay the hide, which Orestes does with impressive dispatch. Aegisthus then examines the entrails, a form of prophetic inquiry ('haruspicy') where the appearance of the animal's organs can predict the future. Horrified at the deformed innards, Aegisthus confesses his fear of Agamemnon's son, but Orestes reassures the king. Asking for a cleaver, Orestes smashes the animal's breastbone. When Aegisthus inspects the newly exposed viscera, Orestes brings the cleaver down on the tyrant's back: 'His entire body, from head to toe, / convulsed in a bloody agony of death' (842–43). Identifying himself as Agamemnon's son, Orestes wins over Aegisthus's slaves, who welcome his return. The Messenger announces that Orestes is on his way, bringing not the gorgon's head, but Aegisthus. Orestes' servant then leaves the way he entered, through an *eisodos*.

15. *Celebration* (Chorus, Electra 859–79)
In a short lyric section, the Chorus praise Orestes for winning a victory greater than the Olympic games. Between the *strophê* and *antistrophê*, Electra invokes the sun, the earth, and the night in celebration, recalling her earlier prayer to the night sky (lines 54–63). She leaves the stage to bring garlands from the cottage to crown Orestes with a victory wreath, while the Chorus continue their joyful dance.

16. *Orestes the victor* (Electra, Orestes [Pylades, servants, perhaps one
    of Aegisthus's men who now supports Orestes, Chorus] 880–906)
As Electra returns with the wreaths, Orestes, Pylades, and servants enter through an *eisodos*, bearing the corpse of Aegisthus. Electra lauds her brother for his victory, garlanding his head, and she does the same for Pylades. Crediting the gods for his triumph, Orestes announces that he has brought back Aegisthus's body as proof of his success. He encourages Electra to revile the corpse, to throw it out for wild beasts to devour, to treat it however she pleases, for she is now Aegisthus's master.

17. *Vaunting over the corpse* (Electra, Orestes [Pylades, Chorus,
    servants] 907–61)
After a moment's hesitation, Electra unleashes a vicious diatribe over the body of Aegisthus, and possibly to his decapitated head.[17] She blames him for destroying her life, orphaning her of her father and her brother. She reviles him as the cowardly butcher of her father, a dangerous seducer of women, a lady's man too handsome for his own good, an effeminate pretender whose fame depended on his wife, and whose sons were 'momma's boys'. Marrying above his station (even

though his wife was a whore), Aegisthus foolishly believed that wealth could buy good character, the sort of unmanly man Electra would never consider for her own husband (948–51). Electra proclaims justice the ultimate victor, a view echoed in the two lines of the Chorus. Orestes tells Pylades and servants to hide Aegisthus's corpse inside the cottage, and they do so, bringing the third movement to a close.

Fourth movement (962 – 1146)

18. *Up next: Clytemnestra* (Electra, Orestes [Chorus] 962–87)
As if on cue, Electra spies Clytemnestra approaching from a distance. Expressing his reservations about killing 'the woman who bore and raised me' (969), Orestes questions the wisdom of Apollo's prophecy that commanded the matricide. Defending the Delphic oracle and accusing her brother of cowardice, Electra shames him into entering the cottage, where he lies in wait for their unsuspecting mother.

19. *Mother and daughter* (Chorus, Clytemnestra, Electra [male attendants, Trojan slave women] 988–1146)
Clytemnestra arrives in the *orchêstra* on a horse-drawn wagon, driven or led by two male servants, and accompanied by her Trojan slaves. The Chorus offer a darkly ironic welcome (988–97), praising the queen for her wealth and good fortune. When Clytemnestra asks her slaves to help her from the carriage, Electra offers her hand instead. She claims she is no less a slave than the Trojan women in her mother's entourage.

Clytemnestra then delivers a thirty-nine-line speech, explaining why she killed Agamemnon. He had lured their daughter Iphigenia to Aulis for a purported marriage to Achilles, only to sacrifice her so the Greeks could sail for Troy and recover the unfaithful Helen. Coming home from the war, he 'installed' (1033) the Trojan prophetess Cassandra in their marriage bed, prompting Clytemnestra to look elsewhere for comfort. Had the situation been reversed – if Menelaus had been abducted and Clytemnestra had sacrificed Orestes to get her brother-in-law back from Troy – Agamemnon would have killed her on the spot. Resting her case, Clytemnestra invites Electra to respond.

To mark the change in speakers, the Chorus leader offers a brief comment, claiming that a wife must always defer to her husband.

Fig. 3 Elektra (Irene Pappas), Clytemnestra (Aleka Katseli), Chorus, and Trojan slaves, from *Elektra* (1962), directed by Michael Cacoyannis. Courtesy of the Michael Cacoyannis Foundation.

Electra then launches a thirty-nine-line rebuttal of her mother. As noted in Chapter 1, the equal lengths suggest the equally timed speeches of plaintiff and defendant in fifth-century Athenian law courts. Electra assails the moral failings of Clytemnestra and compares her to her sister Helen, who brought shame on their brothers Castor and Polydeuces. She accuses her mother of dolling herself up when Agamemnon left for Troy, and of rejoicing when the news from Troy looked bad for the Greeks, because she preferred the lightweight Aegisthus to her warrior husband. Even if she had valid reasons for hating Agamemnon, Clytemnestra had no right to take it out on Electra and Orestes. If she were justified in murdering Agamemnon, then Electra and Orestes have every right to kill her in return.

In a brief dialogue, Clytemnestra understands why Electra sides with Agamemnon: 'Some children prefer the male, / others love their mother more than their father' (1103–4), a subject we will explore in Chapter 7. Expressing regret at killing her husband, Clytemnestra confesses that her fear of Orestes made her defend Aegisthus's harsh measures against her son. Unmoved, Electra denounces the tyrant for supplanting her and Orestes. In a chilling *double-entendre*, she tells her mother that 'even now he dwells in my house' (1120), reminding the audience that his corpse lies hidden inside the cottage.

Clytemnestra enquires about her (ostensible) grandchild, whom Electra claims she delivered without a midwife. Ignorant of the appropriate birth rituals, she asks her mother to enter the cottage and help. The queen tells her slaves to take the carriage away and feed the horses. After the rituals here, she will join Aegisthus at his sacrifice to the Nymphs. The Trojan slaves and attendants exit via an *eisodos* with the horses and wagon.

As Clytemnestra enters the cottage, Electra warns her not to soil her beautiful clothes on the soot-stained walls. Referring to the sacrifice ahead, Electra invokes the knife sharpened not for a calf but for her human victim. She recalls her own 'wedding to death' (line 247) by condemning her mother to a similar fate: 'You will lie beside the man you slept with [Aegisthus] as his bride / in the house of Hades' (1144–45). Electra exits into the cottage, ending the longest scene in the play.

Fifth movement (1147–1359)

20. *The ebb and flow of justice* (Chorus, Clytemnestra from offstage 1147–76)

After Electra's exit, the Chorus perform their third *stasimon*, addressing the changing fortunes of the house of Atreus. In the *strophê* they sing of Agamemnon's death in the bath, his cries echoing through the palace; the *antistrophê* describes Clytemnestra's lioness-like cruelty in slaying him, and the justice that lies ahead. Clytemnestra's offstage cries follow: 'My children, before the gods, don't kill your mother!' (1165). While pitying her fate, the Chorus see divine justice at work, and they announce the appearance of the corpses of Aegisthus and

Clytemnestra on the *ekkuklêma*: 'There is not now, nor ever has there
been / a house more wretched than the race of Tantalus' (1175–76).[18]

21. *Revulsion* (Orestes, Electra, Chorus [Pylades, corpses of Aegisthus
    and Clytemnestra] 1177–232)
Along with the bodies of their victims, the bloodstained brother and
sister enter from the cottage, accompanied by the silent Pylades. In a
kommos (shared lyric), they recreate the matricide, somewhat like
messengers in lyric mode, following this pattern: Orestes, Electra,
Chorus (first strophic pair); Orestes, Chorus (second strophic pair);
Orestes, Electra (third strophic pair). Appalled by the deed and the
oracle that commanded it, Orestes fears that the matricide will make
him a pariah. Repenting her hatred of her mother, Electra grieves that
no husband will take her as a wife. The Chorus claim justice has been
done, but they fault Electra for driving her brother to murder. Orestes
describes how Clytemnestra begged for mercy, baring her breast and
exposing 'the limbs that gave me birth' (1209). Only by covering his
eyes could he drive his sword into her neck. Electra confesses that she
urged her brother on, putting her own hand to the blade. They cover
their mother with a robe, part of the ritual preparation for her burial.

22. *Gods on high* (Chorus, Castor, [Polydeuces], Orestes, Electra,
    [Pylades, corpses of Aegisthus and Clytemnestra] 1233–91)
The Chorus announce the unexpected arrival of two divinities (1233–
37), the deified brothers of Clytemnestra, Castor and Polydeuces. They
descend via the *mêchanê* onto the roof of the cottage (i.e. the *skênê*
building). Addressing Orestes in a monologue (the same number of
lines as the Farmer's opening prologue), Castor tries to bring comfort
and closure. He proclaims that Clytemnestra's fate was just, but that the
matricide was not, blaming 'wise' Apollo's 'unwise' oracle (1246). He
instructs Orestes to give Electra to Pylades in marriage and then flee to
Athens, driven mad by the Furies, chthonic spirits who avenge kindred
bloodshed. The goddess Athena will protect Orestes from these spirits
with her gorgon shield, when he stands trial for murder on the
Areopagus (the 'Hill of Ares', close to the Acropolis). Because Apollo
takes responsibility for the matricide, the jury's votes will divide
equally, setting the precedent that a split verdict guarantees the

defendant's acquittal. The angry Furies will sink into a chasm, establishing an oracle near the Hill of Ares, and Orestes will leave to found an eponymous city in Arcadia.[19]

Castor announces that the citizens of Argos will bury Aegisthus. Clytemnestra will receive funeral rites from Menelaus (just back after the sack of Troy) and his wife Helen (who lived in Egypt throughout the war). Helen never went to Troy. Zeus sent a false image of her to Priam's city in order to unleash 'strife and the slaughter of mortals' (1282). Following this revelation, Castor tells Orestes to let Pylades return to his home in Phocis with Electra 'as virgin and wife' (1284). The new couple will take the Farmer with them, and make him a wealthy man. Ending his monologue, Castor reminds Orestes that he must flee to Athens, stand trial, and then find happiness.

23. *Mortal and immortal perspectives* (Orestes, Castor, Electra, Chorus [Polydeuces, Pylades, corpses of Aegisthus and Clytemnestra] 1292–359)

Orestes and Electra challenge the happy ending outlined by their star-dwelling uncle. Why would the gods allow – and in the case of Apollo, encourage – the murder of their mother? Castor responds that the troubles of the house stem from their ancestors, making their own fate inescapable. Brother and sister embrace in grief, lamenting their separation, their exile from Argos, and loss of their family home. Castor encourages a more positive view, but admits to feeling pity for struggling mortals. Announcing the imminent approach of the Furies who will hound Orestes, Castor takes his leave with his brother on the *mêchanê*, heading for the sea around Sicily to rescue ships and to help those 'who love / piety and justice' (1351–52). The Chorus bid the gods farewell, and the play ends with everyone exiting out the two *eisodoi*.

Euripides' *Electra* and Myth

Reflecting and Re-fashioning Tradition

Tragic myths like those of Electra and Orestes tap into a deep reservoir of archetypal behaviour, delivering larger-than-life stories of passion, error, triumph, grief, and other 'slings and arrows of outrageous fortune', as Shakespeare's Hamlet puts it. Strong external forces – gods, fate, circumstance – can play a decisive role in these stories, exposing human limitations and testing human endurance. Manifest in almost all aspects of ancient Greek culture – epic, tragedy, lyric poetry, philosophy, history, architectural sculpture, vase painting – myths provide guidance, insight, and warning. Although deeply rooted in tradition, their power lies in their flexibility rather than their allegiance to an ideal or perfected version. With a remarkable capacity to incorporate new elements and manipulate old ones, myths thrive on variation, from subtle changes in detail to major twists in their plots. We find this combination of tradition and invention at work in Euripides' *Electra*.[1]

The saga of the house of Atreus makes its earliest appearance in Homeric epic.[2] We meet Agamemnon, Menelaus, and Helen in the *Iliad*, and we hear of Orestes, Electra, Aegisthus, and Clytemnestra in the *Odyssey*. In the later poem, Aegisthus's murder of Agamemnon angers the gods on Olympus, for it epitomizes the refusal of mortals to obey divine commands. Odysseus encounters the spirit of Agamemnon in the underworld, where the murdered Greek leader recounts his death at the hands of Aegisthus, cheered on by Clytemnestra, who ignores her husband's cries for mercy. By avenging Agamemnon's murder, Orestes provides a model for Odysseus's son Telemachus, who faces a horde of suitors that have occupied his father's palace on Ithaca and are plotting Odysseus's death, should he ever return from Troy.[3]

The story also appears in the Epic Cycle, an assortment of shorter epic poems known primarily through later prose summaries. The *Cypria* ('stories connected to Aphrodite') includes the sacrifice of Iphigenia, a significant addition to the Homeric account, and one used later by all the tragedians to justify Clytemnestra's hatred of her husband. Another poem in the Epic Cycle, *Nostoi* ('Homecomings'), credits both Aegisthus and Clytemnestra for killing Agamemnon, and also introduces Pylades as Orestes' ally. The lyric poet Xanthus (*c.* 600 BC) explains that the name Laodikê (mentioned in the *Iliad* as one of Agamemnon and Clytemnestra's daughters) was changed to 'Electra' because Aegisthus and Clytemnestra prevented her from marrying. An ageing virgin, she was 'without a marriage bed', *a [ê] + lektron*, or *Êlektra*, an etymology that Euripides exploits in his play.[4]

The early sixth-century lyric poet Stesichorus wrote an *Oresteia* (also lost), which referred to the sacrifice of Iphigenia and to Clytemnestra's role in the murder of Agamemnon. The poem also mentioned Orestes' return from exile, his recognition by Electra (involving a lock of his hair), Clytemnestra's nightmare that precedes her murder, the pursuit of Orestes by the Furies, and Apollo's help in releasing him from their curse. In one of his epinician odes (*Pythian* 11.15–37), Pindar approaches the story through the character of Pylades. His father Strophius took in Orestes when a nurse saved the young boy from Clytemnestra, after she had murdered Agamemnon and Cassandra. Like the tragedians, Pindar (a younger contemporary of Aeschylus) ponders Clytemnestra's motivation: was it the sacrifice of Iphigenia that drove her to kill her husband, or her desire for Aegisthus?

In his *Oresteia*, which competed at the City Dionysia in 458 BC, Aeschylus weaves these elements together in an integrated trilogy. The first play, *Agamemnon*, describes Agamemnon's sacrifice of Iphigenia, an offering demanded by the goddess Artemis if the Greeks were to capture Troy. After the war, Clytemnestra welcomes her husband home, laying out the woven wealth of the house for him to trample as he enters the palace. Clytemnestra then murders Agamemnon in the bath, and she also kills Cassandra, his war-prize from Troy. Altering the Homeric account, Aeschylus makes Clytemnestra the sole killer; Aegisthus appears only after the fact, celebrating Agamemnon's death as belated justice for his father Thyestes and his brothers. Thyestes unknowingly ate his children (all save Aegisthus) in a horrific feast prepared by *his* brother Atreus, the father of Agamemnon.

The second play of the trilogy, *Choephori* (*Libation Bearers*), deals directly with the subject of Euripides' *Electra*. The play opens at Agamemnon's tomb, where the exiled Orestes has returned to make offerings and plan his revenge. Electra and the Chorus approach with libations sent by Clytemnestra to placate Agamemnon's spirit, following a terrifying nightmare in which she gave birth to a snake that sucked blood from her breast. Orestes reveals himself, proving his identity to Electra by the similarity of their hair and feet, and by a woven garment she gave him in his youth. Prompted by Apollo's oracle, he lays out his plan. Sending Electra back to the palace (she never appears again), he and Pylades arrive disguised as messengers bringing news of Orestes' death. Clytemnestra welcomes them and sends for Aegisthus, whom Orestes kills without difficulty. When he confronts Clytemnestra onstage, however, she bares her breast and begs for life. Orestes hesitates, until Pylades (silent up to this point) tells him to obey Apollo, no matter what. After the offstage matricide, Orestes appears on the *ekkuklêma* with the corpses of his two victims. At the sight of the Furies, whom only he can see, he flees in terror out of the theatre.

The final play, *Eumenides*, begins with Orestes at the *omphalos* (the 'navel of the earth') in Apollo's temple at Delphi, where he seeks asylum from the Furies. Apollo sends him to Athens to stand trial for matricide at a new civic court established by Athena. Apollo appears on Orestes' behalf, and half the jurors vote for acquittal, half for conviction. Athena provides the casting vote, freeing Orestes to return to Argos. The irate Furies threaten the city with destruction, until Athena convinces them to take up residence in Athens with full ritual honours.

Many in the original audience of Euripides' *Electra* would have known the *Oresteia*, which exerted a pronounced influence on the artistic life of Athens,[5] and it left its impact on Euripides and Sophocles. Each wrote an *Electra* that incorporated important elements from Aeschylus's trilogy.[6] However, they chose to put Electra centre-stage and view the story from her perspective: the murder of her father, her mother's betrayal of Agamemnon and marriage to Aegisthus, the tyrant's despotic control over her life, the absence and eventual return of her brother Orestes, her role in the matricide, and her reactions after the murder.

We cannot understand Euripides' *Electra* if we fail to take Aeschylus's *Oresteia* into account. For a start, the recognition scene in Euripides (*El.* 518–78), discussed in Chapter 2, consciously parodies the scene in *Choephori*.[7] The evidence of Orestes' return – a lock of hair, footprints, childhood weaving[8] – strike Electra as nonsensical. She thinks the Old Man has lost his mind, until she, too, sees the scar above her brother's eye.[9] Why does Euripides give us this odd, roundabout recognition scene? Is he indulging in an insider's theatre joke about Aeschylus's dramaturgy, or is something more at stake?

The mismatch between the Old Man's enthusiastic certainty and Electra's growing incredulity looks like the stuff of comedy, and on more than one occasion (in this scene, and elsewhere) Euripides encourages his audience to laugh.[10] For all the humour, however, the Old Man gets it right – Orestes left tokens at Agamemnon's grave, he has returned from exile, he is standing in front of his sister. The forced recognition speaks volumes about Orestes, who could have identified himself in his first scene with Electra, when he learns that she longs to avenge their father, and that the Farmer and Chorus are on her side. For her part, Electra holds such an idealized image of her brother – a man's man, trained in wrestling schools, a warrior who would never return in secret – that she fails to recognize the person with whom she shares the stage for some 200 lines (the Old Man identifies Orestes almost on sight). In the recognition scene, Euripides exposes how far his two main characters have grown apart, failing to fill the heroic contours of their Aeschylean predecessors.

As noted above, Euripides departs from tradition by moving his play to an isolated mountain farm far from the palace of Argos. Electra lives there with her husband, wedded in name only, caught in limbo between virgin and wife. In Aeschylus's *Choephori*, Electra hints at her limited nuptial prospects (A. *Ch.* 132–35, 445–49), and Sophocles in his *Electra* goes further. His Aegisthus will not allow Electra or her sister Chrysothemis to marry, fearing they might give birth to a potential avenger (S. *El.* 959–66). Running with this idea, Euripides has Aegisthus marry Electra to a poor farmer, guaranteeing that no child from their union could possess the status to make a claim on the throne.

Electra remembers the palace as the home she has lost and as the place of her father's murder: 'Destroyed in a meshed web / of deceit ... / ... / you bathed yourself for the last time' (Eur. *El.* 154–57). In both Aeschylus and Sophocles, Orestes avenges his father's murder by slaying Clytemnestra (and Aegisthus) within those same palace walls. But Euripides alters the scenario, moving the assassination of Aegisthus to the meadow where he pastures his horses, and the murder of Clytemnestra to the Farmer's cottage. As Orestes prepares for the matricide, the Chorus recall how Agamemnon 'fell slain / in the bath', his death cries 'resounding from the ceiling, and the stone cornices of the palace' (1148–50). Moments later they hear Clytemnestra's death cries emanating from within the cottage (1165, 1167). Although juxtaposed verbally, the two murders – Agamemnon's and Clytemnestra's – take place in completely different contexts. By shifting the matricide to the country, Euripides attenuates the sense of natural justice that might arise if Clytemnestra were killed in the same place where she had killed her husband.[11]

The continuity of the murder scenes in Aeschylus and Sophocles emphasizes the importance of genealogy, political power, and dynastic inheritance. After the trial in Aeschylus's *Eumenides*, Orestes leaves for Argos knowing that he will return as king and master of his house. At the end of Sophocles' *Electra*, Orestes returns to the palace in Argos and restores his rightful rule. In Euripides' *Electra*, however, Orestes never gets near the palace, even after the matricide. Castor informs him that he must accept permanent exile from Argos and found a new city in Arcadia. Electra, too, never returns home, departing for Phocis with her new husband Pylades. The initial 'displacement' of the setting away from the palace mirrors the banishment of Electra and Orestes at the end of the play. Euripides denies the restoration of political rule and dynastic line found in Homer, Aeschylus, and Sophocles. In their place, loss, remorse, and exile are all that remain of an ancient legacy.[12]

By looking at scenes of arrival and welcome, we can appreciate other ways that Euripides has re-shaped the tradition. Tragedy knows no more memorable scene than Clytemnestra's homecoming for her husband in Aeschylus's *Agamemnon*, with the blood-red fabrics spread out before him, leading into the palace. Aeschylus slyly refers back to this scene in *Choephori*, when Clytemnestra welcomes Orestes and Pylades with the promise of a warm bath and appropriate hospitality (A. *Cho.* 707–15). In similar fashion, Clytemnestra in Sophocles' *Electra* welcomes the unrecognized Tutor (S. *El.* 800–3), convinced by his fictitious account of Orestes' death. Then Orestes and Pylades (both unrecognized) bring the funeral urn with the dead man's ashes into the palace, where they dispatch Clytemnestra with ease. In both Aeschylus and Sophocles' versions, Orestes manoeuvres a welcome into the palace through the ruse of his own death. Nothing like this happens in Euripides' play.

Working intricate variations on his predecessors, Euripides presents four welcoming scenes in *Electra*. When the Farmer returns from his fields and learns that the strangers talking to his wife bring word from Orestes, he greets them warmly: 'Why weren't the doors [literally 'gates'] opened long ago? / Go inside, please … / Accept what hospitality my house can offer' (Eur. *El.* 357–59). The disguised Orestes reluctantly accepts the Farmer's invitation, but he wishes he were in one of the other versions of his story: 'I wish that your brother, flush with prosperity, / were leading me into his more prosperous home' (397–98).[13]

The second welcoming scene (reported by the Messenger) involves Aegisthus's spontaneous invitation that Orestes and Pylades join his sacrifice and feast (Eur. *El.* 779–89). A bullock is brought in, prepared, slaughtered, and flayed, this last action performed by Orestes at his host's behest. Only after the animal's death does the murder of the unsuspecting Aegisthus take place, while he bends over the entrails to examine the omens. The sacrificial context of this scene recalls Clytemnestra's 'welcome' to Cassandra in Aeschylus's *Agamemnon*: 'You, too, Cassandra, come inside . . . / and stand with the other slaves / when we sacrifice at the altar . . . / The beasts stand ready . . . / the altar fires burn' (A. *Ag.* 1035–38, 1056–57). In Aeschylus, Clytemnestra's sacrifice provides the cover for murdering those she has welcomed. Euripides gives us a full-scale sacrifice, but one where the host meets his death at the hands of his guest.

The third welcome takes place onstage when Electra celebrates Orestes' return as a conquering hero (Eur. *El.* 880–89). She crowns her brother and Pylades with garlands (*stephanoi*), a ritual associated with victory at the Panhellenic games, and repeated on the athlete's return to his home city. Electra's welcome of her brother recalls the greeting Agamemnon *should* have received when he returned from Troy: 'It was not with a crown or victory wreaths (*stephanoi*) / that your wife welcomed you home, / but with a two-edged sword' (162–64). In Aeschylus's *Agamemnon*, the Argive king returns bringing visible evidence of his Trojan victory, namely the Trojan princess Cassandra. In Euripides' *Electra*, Orestes also brings a token of his conquest, the mangled body of Aegisthus.

In the final welcoming scene, Electra greets her mother on her arrival at the Farmer's cottage. Again Euripides evokes the homecoming sequence in Aeschylus's *Agamemnon*, but it is Clytemnestra (not Agamemnon) who arrives in a carriage accompanied by Trojan slaves, and it is her daughter, dressed in rags, who welcomes her. Rather than a path of richly dyed textiles leading to the palace, Clytemnestra must tread cautiously to protect her own garments as she walks into the cottage: 'Be careful / not to stain your royal clothes on the soot-covered walls' (Eur. *El.* 1139–40). As in Aeschylus's play, sacrifice provides the smokescreen for what lies ahead. Clytemnestra exits to perform the purification ritual as her daughter intones, 'You will make the sacrifice you must to the gods. /

The sacred basket is raised; sharp is the knife / that stabbed the bull ...'
(1141–43).

At the end of the play, Euripides refers to – and transforms – other
elements from the *Oresteia*. In the onstage encounter between mother
and son in *Libation Bearers*, Clytemnestra bares her breast to remind
Orestes that she gave him life. He hesitates, and cries out 'What shall I
do?' (*ti drasô*; A. *Cho.* 899), the question that Vernant identifies as 'the
fundamental problem of tragedy'.[14] Silent to that point, Pylades tells his
friend to obey Apollo's oracle (A. *Cho.* 900–2), and Orestes forces his
mother into the palace to kill her. In his *Electra*, Euripides denies
Orestes an onstage scene with his mother. But he does ask the same
'tragic question' as his Aeschylean predecessor, only earlier, in the
decisive scene with his sister: 'What shall we do (*ti ... drômen*)? Shall
we kill our mother?' (Eur. *El.* 967). Pylades says nothing; it is Electra
who tells Orestes to follow the oracle: 'If Apollo is foolish, then who is
wise?' (972). Bowing to his sister's will, Orestes utters the tragic words,
'So I will do something terrible' (*kai deina drasô*, 986).

Following the matricide, brother and sister appear with the bodies of
Clytemnestra and Aegisthus on the *ekkuklêma*, recalling the end of
Aeschylus's *Libation Bearers*. In that play, Orestes focuses on the
righteousness of his action, laying out the net that Clytemnestra used to
trap Agamemnon for all to see. In Euripides' version, the killers express
horror and regret at what they have done, covering their mother's corpse
with Orestes' cloak to hide it from sight. Suddenly, Castor appears *ex
machina*, speaking ambiguously of the god whose oracle had pressed for
the matricide: 'What she [your mother] received was just, but what you
did was not. / Apollo, Apollo ... No, he is my lord, and I will keep silent.
/ Although a wise (*sophos*) god, his oracle was not wise (*ouk ... sopha*)'
(Eur. *El.* 1244–46). Castor then explains what lies ahead for Orestes,
summarizing the action of Aeschylus's *Eumenides* in only twenty lines
(Eur. *El.* 1252–72), as if he were on amphetamines.

By incorporating so many elements from *Eumenides* in his account
of Orestes' trial in Athens, Euripides encourages us to compare the
ending he gives his play to that of Aeschylus. After Athena's vote frees

Orestes in *Eumenides*, the Furies threaten to devastate Athens, spreading plague on the land, blasting the crops and animals, destroying the earth's productivity (A. *Eum.* 778–92, 808–22). Athena persuades them to calm their anger and make their home in Athens, honoured by ritual offerings at marriage and childbirth. Aeschylus has the now-transformed Eumenides ('Kindly Spirits') sing a blessing over the city they had planned to ruin: 'May no fierce blast destroy the trees, / ... / no blazing heat blind the flowers / ... / Let flocks fatten / and the earth swell, / .... / a rich yield that honors the gods' (A. *Eum.* 938–48).

At the end of Euripides' *Electra*, Castor makes several efforts to brighten the mood, but he can offer nothing like the uplifting vision of fertility that brings *Eumenides* to a close. We do find a thematic resonance, however, in Euripides' decision to set *Electra* on a rural farm. Recall that the play opens with the Farmer addressing the land – 'O ancient plain of Pelasgian land (*gês*), watered by the river Inachus ...' (*El.* 1), and variations of the word 'earth' (*gê*) occur frequently.[15] At the end of his prologue the Farmer re-asserts his connection to the soil: 'When day breaks, / I'll drive the oxen to the fields to plow and sow my crops. / For a loafer soon learns: prayers to the gods may fill / your mouth, but it's work that fills your stomach' (78–81).

The Farmer's dependence on the earth's productivity suggests an implicit relationship to the blessings sung by the Furies at the end of *Eumenides*. Euripides scatters references to harvests, crops, livestock, and fertility across the play. Reaching his home 'after ten harvests' (*deketesin sporaisin, El.* 1152–53),[16] Agamemnon is cut down in his bath. We see the land's productivity when the Old Man arrives with a lamb, cheese, and wine to feed the visitors (493–99). Aegisthus sacrifices to the Nymphs (nature goddesses linked to water and fertility) in the meadows where he pastures his horses (623–27). Clytemnestra enters the *orchêstra* in a horse-drawn wagon (965, 998–99), and she instructs her slaves to graze the animals while she helps Electra with her ritual (1135–38). Orestes sacrifices a lamb to honour Agamemnon's tomb (90–92, 513–14), and we hear of the bullock that Aegisthus offers to the Nymphs (625–27, 785–86, 811).[17]

While calling attention to the importance of animals, agriculture, and the earth, Euripides foregoes the grand beneficence that ends Aeschylus's *Eumenides*. Unlike the earthbound Furies who guarantee the prosperity of Athens, Castor (who dwells in the stars) makes little reference to the city of Argos and its wellbeing. However, he does inform Orestes that the Furies will deliver a 'harvest of sharp pain' (*deinôn odunôn karpon, El.* 1346). As for the soil and its productivity, the play ends with two corpses in front of a soon-to-be-abandoned farmhouse. We can only imagine what the Farmer would make of his cottage should he return, finding it spattered with a mother's blood spilled by his virgin wife and by the guest he had welcomed so graciously into his home.

We have focused on the interconnections between Aeschylus's *Oresteia* and *Electra* because of the obvious impact of the trilogy on Euripides' play. But Euripides also drew on other versions of the myth – Homer, the epic cycle, Stesichorus, and possibly Sophocles, whose *Electra* may have premiered at the City Dionysia around the time of Euripides' play. Given the uncertainty in dating the two *Electra*'s, we cannot be sure which way the influences flowed. But let us assume for the moment that Sophocles' *Electra* preceded Euripides' play and consider how the younger playwright might have exploited the more original elements in Sophocles' tragedy.[18]

Unlike Aeschylus, whose interest lies in Orestes, Sophocles focuses on Electra (onstage for all but a hundred lines), living a tortured existence under the same roof as her father's assassins. Hoping for Orestes' return, Electra refuses to join her sister Chrysothemis (a Sophoclean innovation), who compromises with the powers that be. When the Messenger brings the (false) news of Orestes' death in a chariot race (discussed in Chapter 1), Electra learns of the loss of her brother. Arriving with the urn ostensibly containing the ashes of the dead hero, Orestes reveals himself to Electra. Once inside the palace, he kills Clytemnestra and then brings her covered corpse onstage to trick Aegisthus, who thinks the body is that of Orestes. When the tyrant learns the truth, Orestes and Pylades force him into the palace to kill him, urged on by a gleefully vindictive Electra, who wants Orestes to expose Aegisthus's corpse rather than bury it. The play ends with no mention of the Furies haunting Orestes for matricide, or of his trial and acquittal in Athens.

The recognition scene in Sophocles offers a useful point of comparison with Euripides' version. When Orestes and Pylades arrive with the urn, Electra clings to it in grief and will not let go. Only by producing his father's signet ring can Orestes persuade her of his identity. Electra's joy knows no bounds, and the Tutor must quiet her so as not to jeopardize their plan. In contrast to Sophocles' exuberant scene, the recognition in Euripides is muted and occurs against Orestes' will. The proof of his identity does not depend on any link to his father (no signet ring) but on a childhood accident. No urn figures in the process, although Euripides does introduce its visual echo in the water jar that Electra carries earlier in the play. Rather than the ritual vessel her Sophoclean counterpart refuses to relinquish, Electra insists on putting down her water jug so that she can mourn her father's fate (Eur. *El.* 140–42), a lamentation that her brother observes in hiding.[19]

Sophocles' Orestes appears cold-blooded, efficient, and without regret, the polar opposite of Euripides' character, so cautious and unsure of the matricide. Both playwrights focus on the psychic damage done to their heroine, but Sophocles' Electra torments her mother with her aggravating presence. Mired in the countryside, Euripides' Electra never sees her mother and longs for her former palace life. She must invent a reason for Clytemnestra to visit her, and when she arrives, we meet both a vain Queen and an apologetic mother, who feels regret for her actions. By contrast, Sophocles' Clytemnestra rails at her daughter: 'You godless, hateful thing! Are you the only person / whose father has died? Does no other human being / feel grief? Go to hell and suffer, / and may the gods below never free you from your lamentations' (S. *El.* 289–92). As for the matricide, the heart of Aeschylus's *Choephori*, Sophocles defangs it, making the death of Aegisthus the climax of his play. Euripides does the reverse, emphasizing the horror of Clytemnestra's killing and her children's appalled reaction to what they did.

We have looked at important sources for Euripides' *Electra* and seen how the playwright incorporates, undermines, and transforms earlier treatments of the story. In Chapter 8 we will return to his apparent assault on the mythical foundations of the story. As his *Electra* amply demonstrates, Euripides was a master of the tragic tradition, and he shaped it in ways that would be hard to imagine without his plays to show us how it's done.

4

In Order of Appearance

Characters (and Actors) in *Electra*

'*As a drama of character, Electra is supreme*
... undoubtedly Euripides' masterpiece'.[1]

As noted in Chapter 2, Aristotle emphasizes the primacy of plot in Greek tragedy. The tendency in contemporary theatre to focus on characters and their idiosyncrasies at the expense of dramatic structure fits well with the late-capitalist celebration of the 'individual' as a locus of consumption and narcissistic self-interest. Other contemporary performance practices – 'post-dramatic' theatre, performance art, endurance art, and the like – often eliminate plot and dramatic roles altogether. Replacing fictional characters with the performer who 'plays' him or her self, these performance pieces follow Aristotle's sensible formula of 'beginning, middle and end'[2] only in the loosest temporal sense: something wasn't happening (or no one was there to see it); then it was happening (or someone came to witness it); and then it wasn't happening any longer (or whoever came, left).[3]

Ancient Greek playwrights worked in a very different environment, where mythical stories helped shape the political and ethical life of the *polis*. As we saw in the previous chapter, the tragedians approached legendary heroes and heroines from different angles and directed their narratives towards different ends. In *Electra*, Euripides alters the contours and motivations of those characters that appear in Aeschylus and Sophocles (Electra, Orestes, Pylades, the old Tutor, Clytemnestra, Aegisthus) and introduces others (the Farmer, Castor) to serve the tale he wants to tell.

Following Aristotle, if the soul of tragedy lies not in the characters *per se* but in their story as structured by the playwright, then to what extent do tragic characters have internal lives independent of the situation in which we find them? As audience members attending Euripides' play, we listen to what Electra says, watch what she does, observe how other characters treat her, and note what they say about her. This information helps us understand what is happening and why, but it does not mean that Electra has a life that can be discovered or analysed apart from the play. The masked male actor who performed Electra at the City Dionysia surely considered the emotions, mood, and motivations of this complicated dramatic figure. However, his performance also would have reflected his knowledge of the play's relationship to prior tradition (Chapter 2), and his mastery of Euripides' language and modes of expression (the subject of our next chapter).

The Greek term *charaktêr* – a 'mark' or 'stamp' that establishes the real thing (such as a coin) from an imitation (a counterfeit) – may help us understand Euripides' approach to dramatic character. Disturbed by the Old Man's scrutiny, Orestes asks his sister, 'Why is he staring at me, as if looking for / the mark (*charaktêr*) of true silver?' (*El.* 558–59).[4] When the Old Man announces that the stranger is really Orestes, Electra responds, 'What mark (*charaktêr*) have you seen that might persuade me?' (572). In spite of Orestes' desire to remain unrecognized, the scar above his eyebrow proves that he is, in fact, himself, and he can no longer pretend otherwise.

Of course, a tragic character cannot be read as easily as an engraved hallmark on a piece of silver. As Goldhill observes, '*Electra* returns again and again to the question of how to evaluate character, a theme that is constructed specifically through an interplay of heroic expectations and human shortcomings.'[5] When the poor Farmer welcomes him into his home, Orestes considers the difficulty of finding a clear way to evaluate nobility of character (*tous eugeneis*, 385).[6] Poverty, wealth, bravery in battle, social status, physical appearance, and ancestry prove inadequate for predicting admirable behaviour. The proof of character lies in what a character does. With this in mind, let us look more closely at the *dramatis personae* and what we learn about them over the course of the play.

The Farmer

The Farmer begins the play by discussing significant events in the life of Electra and her family. Only later does he turn to his own background, born of good Mycenaean stock but now reduced to poverty (*El.* 35–38).[7] Although wedded to Electra, he respects her lineage and her virginity, given that Aegisthus forced the marriage on them. The Farmer conveys all the information the audience needs to follow the story – the mythic 'givens', the innovations of a rural setting and a wedded Electra, and a glimpse at the economic and social disparities that will emerge as the play unfolds.

If this were a modern drama, we might expect 'down-home' vocabulary and rough manners from this man of the soil, but the Farmer only occasionally demonstrates such behaviour. He utters twelve proper names in his first ten lines, and a total of thirty-five in the prologue. He invokes the ancient Pelasgians, the early inhabitants of the plain of Argos, drained by the river Inachos; the great figures of the Trojan War, Agamemnon (named four times) and Priam; Aegisthus (named seven times, and once more as 'son of Thyestes'); Clytemnestra (once by name, once as 'child of Tyndareus'); and of course the principal players, Electra and Orestes (each named three times). The Farmer never names himself, nor does anyone else in the play.

The list of characters (probably not by Euripides) found in the oldest surviving manuscript identifies the Farmer as *Autourgos*, 'a man who works [the land] by himself'. The Farmer talks about the ploughing and the sowing he must undertake, and Electra refers to him as a 'toiler' (75) and their home as 'a day-labourer's cottage' (207). On his arrival at this rough Argive hillside, Orestes expects a 'ploughman' (104) to pass by, and he views the cottage as fit for a 'ditch digger or cowherd' (252). Electra describes her husband as 'a poor but noble man' (*penês anêr gennaios*, 253); the Farmer uses similar language of himself: 'Although a poor man (*penês*), / I am not ignoble by nature' (*êthos dusgenes*, 362–63).[8]

Portrayed as modest and virtuous, the Farmer comes across as a principled 'good guy'. We see this in his sexual abstinence, his recognition that farm drudgery does not suit his wife, his generosity and hospitality, and his regret that he cannot offer more to his guests. He occasionally utters aphorisms of folk wisdom that give us a sense of his world-view. Reflecting traditional Greek country life, the Farmer is shocked to find his wife talking to strangers in front of the cottage, but once he learns that they bring news of Orestes, he welcomes them inside. Deeply embarrassed by their dwelling, Electra harangues him for doing so. He responds, 'If they're as noble as they seem, won't they / gladly take the little we can offer and see it as a lot?' (406–7). Surprising in a Greek tragedy, these exchanges have the ring of everyday domestic encounters, well suited to the rural world of the Farmer. With his departure, this tone never returns, and Euripides re-directs the action towards recognition, revenge, and remorse.

Given the three-actor rule discussed in Chapter 1, we can be fairly sure of the role-divisions in *Electra*. The protagonist played the title role, the second actor played Orestes, and the third actor took on all the other parts: the Farmer, the Old Man, Messenger, Clytemnestra, and Castor. The role of the Old Man does not seem like a stretch for the actor playing the Farmer. Other than age (indicated by posture and mask), they both live and work in the country. But the shift to Clytemnestra speaks volumes about the range and technical mastery of the ancient tragic actor. It forces us to question the deep psychological commitment many modern performers view as the *sine qua non* for playing a tragic role.

Electra

A complex character full of contradictions and idiosyncrasies,[9] Electra remains unwavering in her desire to take vengeance on Aegisthus and Clytemnestra. Her forced marriage to the Farmer, her marginal position as wife and virgin (far stranger in the ancient world than in our own), and the loss of her home and status have taken their toll. Time and again Electra protests the indignities she has suffered, frequently using the Greek term *hubris* to describe what her enemies have done to her. The word has several meanings, including 'physical violation', 'assault', and 'rape', a topic dealt with further in Chapter 7. It seems that Electra's sense of social humiliation motivates her far more than her moral outrage at her father's murder.[10]

Many interpreters of the play note Electra's predilection for self-dramatization. As Denniston puts it, 'One feels throughout the earlier part of the play that she is reveling in her misery'.[11] Given to verbal and physical hyperbole, Electra works herself into a state of oblivious self-concern. On her first entry, she fails even to notice the Farmer (who has been onstage for fifty lines), consumed as she is with showing the gods the misery of her life.[12] She frequently employs rhetorical tropes to make her case, revealing a level of self-awareness underneath her passionate outbursts. She launches a long speech on her life of deprivation and misery with the rhetorically balanced line, 'I should speak if I must, and, since you are friends, so must I speak' (300). At other times, her abrupt tonal shifts seem to come out of nowhere. On her husband's return from the fields, she addresses him with respect: 'Oh dearest one' (345). As soon as Orestes enters the cottage, however, Electra changes her tune: 'Reckless fool' (404), she says, chiding the Farmer for inviting rich guests into their poor home, her embarrassment trumping the norms of hospitality.[13]

Inconsistencies in Electra's behaviour and self-presentation complicate our picture of her. Although her hair is razor-cropped and filthy, she claims it is well combed and feminine. She indicates that her tattered clothes and unkempt appearance keep her from attending the festival, but she rejects the Chorus' offer to loan her the proper clothes and accessories. She grumbles more than once about having to fetch water from the spring, although her husband insists that she need not perform this demeaning task. She tells Orestes that she shuns young women, but the presence of the female Chorus (friends of Electra) suggests otherwise. She implies that Agamemnon has no proper grave, but both Orestes and the Old Man make offerings at his tomb. She urges the strangers to tell Orestes all about her impoverished life and dwelling, but she derides the Farmer for inviting them inside, where they could see for themselves. Electra claims that modesty prohibits her from speaking what she feels about Aegisthus, but then she rails at his corpse, insulting him for being both a feminized weakling and an irresistible seducer of women.

A puzzling aspect of Electra's character involves her occasional moments of panic, suggesting that fear lies closer to the surface than we might expect. At the sight of the strange men near her cottage (Orestes and Pylades in disguise), she flees in terror, an understandable response considering the isolated location of her dwelling. Harder to explain is her vow to commit suicide if Orestes fails to kill Aegisthus. She prepares to carry out her promise until a Messenger arrives, whose identity Electra doubts. When he reassures her that he is her brother's servant (previously onstage with her for almost two hundred lines), Electra acknowledges that fear kept her from recognizing him.[14]

For all these complexities and contradictions, Electra shows single-minded purpose in punishing those who have ruined her life. She decries what Aegisthus has done, exiling her brother, forcing her into a death-like marriage, and denying access to the palace and inheritance that rightly belongs to her and Orestes.[15] Imagining her absent brother as a heroic avenger, she has a hard time accepting that he proves otherwise in the flesh, and at the crucial moment she shames him into committing matricide. In the scene with her mother, Electra's bitter callousness contrasts with Clytemnestra's efforts at reconciliation and her doubts about the course she has taken.

Only after her mother's murder does Electra display any misgivings about the deed, and her horror at what she has done marks an abrupt change: 'I am to blame. / Wretch (*talaina*) that I am, to move like wildfire against my mother! / She bore me as her daughter' (1182–84).[16] Matricide, we might say, brings Electra to her senses. Her belated contrition recalls that of Clytemnestra, who comes to regret what she has done: 'Ah! What a wretch (*talaina*) my plotting has made me! / Much more anger than necessary I drove against my husband' (1109–10). As we shall see in Chapter 9, later versions of Electra's story explore and develop the similarities between mother and daughter.

In an important sense, Euripides' protagonist gets what she thinks she wants. She shows the gods her suffering; she appears as a loving wife (while complaining how wretched her marriage makes her); she browbeats her husband into doing her bidding; she pays Aegisthus back for the outrage he has inflicted; she effectively plots Clytemnestra's murder; she shames Orestes into matricide and joins him in the deed; and she ends up with the kind of husband (Pylades) that befits a princess. For all her success, it is telling that she feels only regret and loss at the close of the play.

By far the largest role, Electra poses great challenges for the actor. Onstage for all but 180 lines, and speaking roughly one-third of the lines in the play, she also sings a monody before the Chorus enter, and joins the young women and Orestes in a shared lyric following the matricide.[17] She has significant interactions with all the major characters: the Farmer, Chorus, Orestes, Old Man, Messenger, Clytemnestra, and Castor. As for those who remain silent, Electra crowns Pylades, reviles the corpse of Aegisthus, and compares herself to the Trojan slave women who accompany Clytemnestra – she too has seen her freedom replaced by servitude.

Electra demonstrates ruthless self-control (the scene with her mother, in which she must act as if she recently gave birth) and indulgent self-pity (her first scene with her brother), scheming resolve (her childbirth fiction) and petty outbursts of emotion (her reaction to her husband, her doubting the Old Man's sanity). At times Electra's anguish and resentment consume her; at other times they seem like useful props in a performance she wants to give to whatever audience might be watching (the gods, the Farmer, the Chorus, Orestes).

Electra is clearly the 'motor' of the play, and a successful production depends on the actor's ability to engage the audience in her anguish over a life that might have been, and her compulsive drive towards vengeance and restitution, which leads – unexpectedly – to deeply affecting remorse.

Orestes

In contrast to his portrayal in Homer, Aeschylus, and Sophocles, Euripides' Orestes appears a most unlikely avenger. Cautious, indecisive, unsure of his next move, he seems like the wrong man for the job. As noted in Chapter 2, Orestes lingers at the border so that he can flee to safety if necessary, and he refuses to reveal himself even when he learns of his sister's absolute commitment to revenge. Only the Old Man's dogged persistence forces Orestes into the light, and even then he must depend on others to plot vengeance on Aegisthus and Clytemnestra.

Behind his caution and indecisiveness, Orestes demonstrates an egotistical arrogance that reflects his aristocratic background. He assumes that the Farmer respects Electra's virginity because he fears her brother, even though Electra tells him otherwise. He perceives Electra's dwelling place as only fit for a ditch digger or cowherd, and he has to steel himself and his entourage to go inside.

If verbal assertion and hyperbole mark his sister, then questions and uncertainty characterize Orestes.[18] By rough count, he makes over seventy inquiries during the course of the play. Some elicit important information he needs to know; others highlight his lack of resolve and reluctance to take charge. He asks the Old Man how to revenge himself on Aegisthus, and he questions the trustworthiness of Apollo's oracle. He initially responds to the Farmer's hospitality not by accepting it, but by considering how one might determine true nobility and judge goodness in another. The problem with Orestes' philosophizing lies not in its irrelevance but in his failure to apply what he says to himself.[19] By contrasting Electra's mythic vision of her brother (too brave to return to Argos in secret) with the less than heroic figure we see onstage, Euripides exposes the gap between noble ideas (and 'ideas about nobility') and their realization.

When Orestes exits to find Aegisthus, we have no idea what he will do or how he will do it. 'I'm ready to go, if someone will show me the way' (*El.* 669) is the last thing Orestes says about the plan, before calling on the gods and Agamemnon for help. Joined by Electra and the Chorus, his invocation brings to mind the great *kommos* in Aeschylus's *Choephori*, but it delivers only 'a faint echo of that powerful, violent, and bloodcurdling scene'.[20] Nonetheless, this short prayer sequence marks the beginning of the change in Orestes' character that we hear about in the Messenger's speech.

In place of the cowardly prevaricator and uncertain plotter, at the sacrifice and feast of Aegisthus we meet a very different Orestes. Quoted several times by the Messenger, he comes across as daring and inventive, quick-witted and cool under pressure, adept and effective when the time is right. Returning to the stage with the body of Aegisthus, Orestes seems transformed, a cold-blooded assassin, crowned like an Olympian champion in a brutal blood sport, urging Electra to abuse the corpse any way she pleases.

The sight of his mother arriving from Argos turns him around again. From the guilt-free, exultant killer of Aegisthus, Orestes reverts to a man haunted by destiny and trying to fight it off: 'How could I kill the woman who bore and raised me?' (969). Earlier, while still in disguise, Orestes asserts that 'only the oracles of Apollo / are steadfast; I bid farewell to human prophecies' (399–400). Now he finds that very oracle 'foolish' (971).[21] He wonders if 'perhaps some demon disguised as the god made the prophecy', but his sister will have none of it: 'Seated at the sacred tripod of Delphi? I don't think so. / ... / Don't you dare get soft and play the coward. / Practice the same deceit you used / when you killed her husband Aegisthus' (979–84).[22] Shamed into acquiescence, Orestes waits inside the cottage while Electra plays cat and mouse with the unsuspecting Clytemnestra.

In resisting what he has to do, Orestes departs radically from other versions of the story. With prescient horror he knows that matricide will mean his exile: 'I was pure before, but I will be exiled for killing my mother' (975). As we will see in the next chapter, Euripides highlights Orestes' miserable life as a fugitive from Aegisthus. An 'exiled man is powerless' (*asthenês ... pheugôn anêr*, 236), he says, and Electra repeats that assessment almost verbatim (*asthenês pheugôn anêr*, 352).

Confirming his worst fear, Orestes learns from Castor that he must suffer banishment from Argos and will never return to his homeland. As the play draws to a close, we see Orestes covered with Clytemnestra's blood, telling his sister, 'Sing a funeral dirge / for me as if at a dead man's tomb' (1325–26). We would not have expected this from the Orestes we first meet, fresh from Delphi, back in the Argive countryside, welcoming 'the shining face of the dawn' (102).

Pylades

Praised by Orestes, the Old Man, and Electra as a loyal friend, the silent Pylades is onstage for a good part of the play, some 750 lines. The original audience may have expected him to speak before the matricide, as he does in Aeschylus's *Choephori*, but Euripides' Pylades remains silent throughout.

With the appearance of the Dioskouroi at the end of the play, however, his character gains new importance. Castor announces that Pylades will marry Electra, taking her home with him to Phocis, along with the Farmer who will find a more prosperous life there. Electra says nothing to her new husband, although both Castor and Orestes urge her to see her future with Pylades in a joyful light. Earlier in the play, Electra praises Pylades effusively when she crowns him and Orestes for murdering Aegisthus: 'And you, comrade in arms, scion of a most righteous father, / Pylades! Accept from my hand this garland, / for you win a prize equal to his / in this contest' (*El.* 886–89). Whatever affection between Electra and Orestes' friend may surface there, we see no evidence of it at the end of the play.[23]

Pylades' silent presence poses challenges and opportunities for a stage director. Does he remain on the margins, lurking in the background? When and how does he make his presence felt? Does Pylades represent a calming influence on Orestes, or an ominous reminder of what lies ahead? How does he enter the stage after Clytemnestra's murder? Would his presence on the *ekkuklêmma* with

Orestes, Electra, and the corpses of Aegisthus and Clytemnestra dilute the dynastic malediction behind the murders? What is his physical relationship with Electra at the end of the play? Do they exit together, or separately? Posing these questions helps us recognize the important role that Pylades (mute though he is) can play in a performance of *Electra*.

The Chorus

The Chorus consists of young female friends of Electra who, like her, live far from the city, and who have come to invite her to join them at the Argive Heraia.[24] They extend Electra their comfort and support, offering her clothes and jewellery so that she can attend the festival, and sympathizing with her when she refuses their request. Electra informs the disguised Orestes that they are loyal and trustworthy, and so they remain throughout the play. When Electra fears that Orestes has failed in his revenge plot, they prevent her from committing suicide, and they join in her celebration for Orestes and Pylades following the murder of Aegisthus. They welcome Clytemnestra to the Farmer's cottage, knowing full well that she walks into a fatal trap. When Electra departs from Argos at the end of the play, she bids the Chorus farewell, calling them 'female citizens' (*polites*, 1335) to emphasize their ties to the city she must leave.[25]

The Chorus's primary contribution to the drama lies in their lyric odes, which extend far beyond their conceivable experience as country maidens. In the first *stasimon*, they invoke the Trojan War, from the lilting departure of the Greek ships to the bloodshed depicted on Achilles' armour. They end their ode abruptly with an image of Clytemnestra paying with her blood for the bloodshed of her husband, the Greek general Agamemnon. In the second *stasimon*, the Chorus recount the legend of the golden lamb, a tale of marital infidelity, palace intrigue, and dynastic politics. In response to the iniquities of the house of Atreus, Zeus changed the course of the sun, disrupting the climate in the known Greek world. Having laid out the myth for the audience (the stage is empty of actors), the Chorus deconstruct it in the final *antistrophê*. They find such stories incredible, for they doubt that the gods would react to the malfeasance of lowly mortals by altering the paths of heavenly bodies. Nonetheless, they admit that such tales encourage humans to honour the gods, precisely what Clytemnestra failed to do when she slew her husband. We will return to this chorus in Chapter 8.

Both odes open with an idyllic setting – flute-loving dolphins gambolling in the ocean, the Argive mountains resounding with Pan's pastoral melodies – only to end in bloodshed, as the Chorus zero in on Clytemnestra's murder of Agamemnon.[26] In the third *stasimon*, they directly evoke his final moments, his screams in the bath as his wife cuts him down with an axe. As if on cue, Clytemnestra's desperate voice cries out from the cottage, confirming the Chorus' confidence that past crimes do not go unpunished. While they believe that Clytemnestra suffered justly, they fault Electra for driving Orestes to commit matricide: 'Friend, you did a terrible thing / to your brother, who wanted no part in it' (1204–5).[27]

Euripides prepares us for the Chorus's change of heart at the end of the play when, in the second *stasimon*, they question the veracity of the myth they have just performed. They draw the audience into the story and then back away from it, forcing us to consider what we've just experienced from a different perspective. Choral self-reference can produce a similar effect. When the Chorus use the language of music, song, and dance to suggest their own performance in the *orchêstra*, they encourage the audience to remain alert to the 'how', as well as the 'what', of the drama. During the *parodos*, for example, they invite Electra to join the festival dance in Argos, but Electra expresses no interest in the 'whirling dance of a virgin chorus' (178–80), a phrase that also applies to the very women to whom she is speaking.

In the first *stasimon*, the Chorus imagine 'the chorus of Nereids' and '*aulos*-loving dolphins' (434–36) that accompany the ships;[28] they marvel at the 'chorus of stars' (467) on Achilles' shield, and the Sphinx with its 'prey-winning song' (471) on his helmet. In the second *stasimon*, they sing of 'Pan's sweet-voiced music, / which he plays on his . . . / reed pipe' (702–4), and they describe the Argive 'choruses' (711) that celebrate the golden lamb. Before the temples, 'a flute, the servant of the Muses, / sang out its lovely melody' (716–17). But then 'a different song rose up' (718), the one that tells of the treachery of Thyestes, who steals the lamb along with Atreus's wife. One song leads to another, one story to another, until both the Chorus and the audience wonder in what way these stories are true, and for what purpose they are being told.

In the short ode after the Messenger speech, the Chorus celebrate Orestes' victory over Aegisthus: 'Let us dance, lifting our feet and leaping / towards heaven like a fawn / . . . / Accompany our chorus / with a triumphant song of victory' (860–65). They urge one another to 'continue our chorus, the dance so loved by the Muses' (875) and to 'let our joyful voices rise with the *aulos*' (879). While calling attention to their own singing and dancing, the Chorus point to another choral performance, the epinician odes that honoured victors at the Panhellenic games (recall that Orestes pretends to be an athlete on his way to Olympia). Although the audience may find themselves swept up in Orestes' triumph, the Chorus's comparison of a brutal murderer to a victorious athlete give us reason to pause. As is often the case in Euripides, the Chorus of *Electra* affects the audience in the theatre as much as the characters and the action onstage.

The Old Man

Performed by the same actor who played the Farmer, the old shepherd brings the rural world back into the play, bearing wine, cheese, plaited garlands, and a lamb to feast the strangers. Like the Chorus whose interest in the festival of Hera quickly vanishes, the Old Man soon forgets the reason for his visit, distracted by his conviction that Orestes has returned. Calling himself a 'shriveled old man', he complains of the climb to Electra's cottage, 'dragging myself up the steep path . . . / with bent back and tottering legs' (*El.* 490–92). Both Electra and Orestes address him as 'old one' (*geraie*, the root of our word 'geriatric'),[29] and Orestes assumes that this 'ancient relic of a man' (554) in tattered clothes must be a slave. Moments later, this 'relic' recognizes Orestes.

The Old Man comes up with a plan that takes advantage of Aegisthus's absence from the palace, advising Orestes to find a way to join the tyrant's ritual celebration in the country. As for Clytemnestra's murder, Electra instructs her old friend to take the news to the palace that she has given birth to a son. Now it is the Old Man who expresses disbelief, doubting that Electra's ploy will work on Clytemnestra. Once the evil genius of Electra's plan sinks in, however, he burns with enthusiasm: 'When I've seen this [Clytemnestra's death], let me die!' (663).[30] With far more energy than when he arrived, the Old Man exits with Orestes and his retinue.[31]

Next to the Corinthian Messenger in *Oedipus Tyrannus*, no other character in Greek tragedy brings so many strands of a plot together. The Old Man comes from Agamemnon's tomb; he recognizes Orestes, who otherwise would never be identified; he thinks of the plan to kill Aegisthus; he is the linchpin in Electra's childbirth ploy, bringing news to Clytemnestra. Like the Farmer before him, the Old Man walks out of the play, but the actor (who has played both of those roles) soon returns as the Messenger.

The Messenger

In most Greek tragedies, the Messenger who reports an offstage event has not appeared onstage before: a terrified shepherd describes the maenads in *Bacchae*; a palace servant reports the hero's madness in *Heracles*; an escaped prisoner narrates Theseus's victory in *Suppliant Women*. In *Electra*, however, the Messenger who arrives must allay Electra's fears: 'Who are you? Why should I trust what you tell me?' (*El.* 765). He proves his *bona fides* by reminding her that he is Orestes' servant, whom she had seen earlier with her brother. At that point, the attendant was a non-speaking role, played by an extra. After Orestes' entourage exits, the actor who played the Old Man changed his mask and costume for those of Orestes' servant, and then he returns as the Messenger who describes Aegisthus's murder.[32]

The personal characteristics of the Messenger in tragedy usually matter very little; the message he delivers is what counts. But as one of Orestes' slaves, the Messenger in *Electra* views his master's victory as a triumph. He employs surprisingly large doses of direct speech (thirty-five out of eighty-four lines), quoting Orestes five times (a total of fifteen lines), probably adopting the vocal inflection of the Orestes' actor. The situation becomes more interesting with Aegisthus, whom the Messenger quotes six times (a total of twenty lines). Because Aegisthus never appears alive onstage, the Messenger could invent the voice of Aegisthus to give us a sense of what that character was like.[33]

Before he arrives, Electra cries out, 'Where are the messengers?' (*pou gar aggeloi*, 759), calling attention to the convention in tragedy of the Messenger speech, a mainstay of Euripdean dramaturgy. Reported news from other sources plays an important role in the plot as well. The Chorus learn of the Argive festival from a mountain man who brings them the news (*aggellei*, 171).[34] The ersatz stranger reports (*aggellein*, 230) that Orestes is alive, and Electra tells him to take back the news (*aggell'*, 303) of her miserable existence to her brother. The Farmer must bring the news (*apaggelô*, 420) about Orestes to the Old Man, news that Clytemnestra would find bitter if reported to her (*aggeilaimen an*, 418). Electra sends the Old Man to her mother with a different message: 'Deliver the news (*apaggell'*) that I have just given birth to a boy' (652). The Old Man assures Electra that the words 'will seem to come out of your own mouth' (667). It is as if the actor playing the Old Man anticipates his upcoming role as the Messenger, when he will quote Orestes and Aegisthus at length.

Aegisthus

Although Aegisthus never appears alive onstage, he remains an important presence.[35] Seven times in the prologue the Farmer singles him out by name, emphasizing his brutal treatment of Orestes and Electra, but also highlighting Aegisthus's fear of Agamemnon's children. The Old Man concurs, describing the tyrant as 'consumed with fear, unable to sleep' (*El.* 617), information that Orestes uses when he joins Aegisthus's sacrifice: 'Do you really fear a plot from some exile / when you rule over the city?' (834–35). Electra gives us a contradictory sense of Aegisthus's character. On the one hand, he seems a drunken buffoon, weak and effeminate, a kept man who owes his status to his wealthy wife. On the other hand, Electra sees him as malevolence personified: her father's murderer, the usurper of Agamemnon's bed and kingdom, the tyrant who drove her brother into exile and who violates her own life.

In the Messenger speech, Aegisthus emerges in a very different light – outgoing, almost jovial, generous and hospitable. He prepares a beautifully observed sacrifice for the Nymphs, inviting the strangers to share the feast and spend the night. He even takes Orestes by the hand, refusing to accept 'no' for an answer. Aegisthus encourages his guest's active participation in the sacrifice, bantering with him about the strangers' (ostensible) Thessalian background. When Aegisthus observes ominous signs in the animal's entrails, his fear begins to mount, until Orestes smashes him through the backbone with a cleaver. Aegisthus's body twitches convulsively as he dies, never knowing who – or what – hit him.[36]

At the end of the play, Castor announces that the 'citizens of Argos / will cover the body of Aegisthus in a grave of earth' (1276–77). This surprising detail gives the impression that his rule was less oppressive to the city at large than to Electra and Orestes, whose mother he seduced and whose father he helped to kill.

Clytemnestra

Euripides' treatment of this tragic figure differs markedly from that of Aeschylus and Sophocles.[37] Aeschylus's Clytemnestra towers over his *Agamemnon* like a force of nature. Passionate, intelligent, and outrageously daring, she kills her husband without help from Aegisthus. Sophocles' Clytemnestra seems mean-spirited and bitter by comparison, in no small part because Electra hounds her relentlessly. In both Aeschylus and Sophocles, a terrifying nightmare prompts Clytemnestra to send libations to calm the spirit of Agamemnon. Euripides' Clytemnestra has no such nightmare and sends no offerings to her husband's grave. We learn from the Farmer that Clytemnestra persuaded Aegisthus not to kill Electra as he originally had planned, suggesting that she still has some maternal feelings for her daughter. She tells Electra straight-out that she regrets her past actions: 'Daughter, don't think / I'm all that happy with the things I've done. / ... / Did I stir up more hatred for my husband than he deserved?' (*El.* 1105–10).

In their scene together, Clytemnestra moves between logic-chopping and heart-felt confession; she expresses a mother's grief over Iphigenia and a tyrant's fear of Orestes; she yearns for rapprochement with her daughter, while longing for the absent Aegisthus. Acknowledging Electra's childhood preference for her father, Clytemnestra feels sympathy for her daughter who gave birth alone, without the help of a midwife or female companions. A more suspicious character might have wondered about the group of women who greet her on her arrival, and who later reject her rationale for murdering Agamemnon: 'What you say is just, but the justice you worked is shameful' (1051). Expecting to meet her grandson as part of her daughter's post-partum purification, Clytemnestra enters the cottage oblivious to the deception that will end her life.

The audience hears her cries from within, as she begs her children not to kill her (1165). When Orestes appears onstage with her corpse, he describes how she bared her breast to him and pleaded for her life. The remorse her children express over her dead body, and Castor's judgement of the folly of Apollo's oracle, lead many to conclude that Clytemnestra's murder was unnecessary and morally reprehensible.

Castor and Polydeuces, the Dioskouroi ('Sons of Zeus')[38]

When Clytemnestra first enters the *orchêstra*, the Chorus welcome her as 'the sister of the noble sons of Zeus, / who dwell among the stars of fiery heaven, / honoured as saviours by men / caught in the sea's roar' (*El.* 990–93). Electra reminds Orestes that the Dioskouroi twins once had been suitors for her hand in marriage (312–13), and she calls Clytemnestra and Helen 'unworthy of their brother Castor' (1064). For all the earlier references to the Dioskouroi, the physical arrival of Castor and Polydeuces *ex machina* ('from the machine') comes as a complete surprise.

The demigods respond to their sister's murder after having 'just calmed a ship-threatening / tempest' (1241–42), and they depart at the end of the play 'for the waters off Sicily, / to rescue ships that sail the deep sea' (1347–48). Scholars once thought that Euripides was alluding to Athens' ill-fated expedition against Sicily in 415 B C, but the uncertainty around *Electra*'s date makes that connection doubtful. The Dioskouroi did have other ties to Sicily and also to Athens, where they were worshipped at the Anakeion sanctuary on the east slope of the Acropolis, around the corner from the theatre of Dionysus.[39]

Raising doubts about the justice of Clytemnestra's murder, Castor criticizes Apollo for the oracle that commanded the matricide.[40] Nevertheless, he predicts a bright future for Orestes, Electra, Pylades, and the Farmer, even though they all must leave Argos. Neither Electra nor Orestes takes comfort at what lies ahead, and Castor finds their grief contagious: 'Even the gods and I myself feel pity for mortals, / all their trials and tribulations' (1329–30). Still, he struggles to make the best of a bad situation, like the fifth-century equivalent of a spin-doctor insisting on a silver lining in the black cloud of matricide.

Whatever glorious future Castor imagines for his nephew and niece, he leaves the audience in a state of shock with his myth-shattering news about the Trojan War. Zeus swept the real Helen off to Egypt and sent a *doppelgänger* in her place, meaning that the war was fought over a phantom. Euripides tells the story more fully in *Helen*, which post-dates *Electra*, and also ends with the Dioskouroi appearing *ex machina*. In that play, Castor (along with his silent twin) safeguards his sister Helen's reunion with her husband Menelaus and guarantees their homecoming to Sparta, an apparently happy conclusion to the devastation of the pointless Trojan conflict.[41] At the end of *Electra*, however, Electra and Orestes face separation and exile, and the revenge they took on their mother seems as unnecessary as the war on Troy waged by their father.

Here is a chart of the probable role divisions for the three actors who created the parts in Euripides' original production at the City Dionysia:

Protagonist (first actor)	Electra
Deuteragonist (second actor)	Orestes (and Messenger?)
Tritagonist (third actor)	Farmer, Tutor, Messenger, Clytemnestra, Castor
Mute actors	Pylades, Polydeuces, servants, corpses of Aegisthus and Clytemnestra

Language

Some theatre historians argue that Greek tragedy arose from a 'song culture', concluding that tragic performances resembled modern opera more than spoken drama.[1] This view fails to take into account the importance of speech, argument, rhetoric, wordplay, poetry, thematic motifs, and the inter-textuality discussed in Chapter 3. One of the great delights of Greek tragedy lies in grappling with the power of language to make a case, establish a character, develop an image, evoke a myth, build suspense, and deepen dramatic conflict. From the broad movement of the plot to the intensity of a single moment, Greek tragedians worked essentially through language, much as Shakespeare did 2,000 years later. We cannot hope to understand a play like *Electra* if we don't look closely at the words and how they work on an audience's imagination to create the world of the play.

Let us begin with the language of colour, not the first thing one thinks of when discussing Greek tragedy. *Electra* abounds with descriptions of colours and hues, from the 'dark blue prows' (436) of the Greek ships sailing for Troy to the 'snake-armed, black skinned' Furies (1345) that pursue Orestes on his way to Athens. At Aegisthus's sacrifice and feast, Orestes lays bare with a knife the 'white flesh under the calf's skin' (823); Clytemnestra imagines Iphigenia stretched over the altar for Agamemnon to 'slit her pale white throat' (1023). Colour-inflected language enhances an audience's ability to see these events in the mind's eye, even though none of them actually takes place onstage.

Electra enters the play addressing the 'black night that suckles the golden stars' (54), and Orestes speaks of the 'white face of dawn' (102). The Chorus sing of the 'burning circle of the sun' on Achilles' shield (464–65), the 'shining day' of Orestes' return (585–86), the 'light of the sun' with its 'hot golden face' (729, 739–40), the 'bright path of the stars'

(727–28), and the 'pale visage of dawn' (730–31). These evocative phrases support the temporal arc of the play, but they also inform the Chorus's account of the sun reversing its course across the sky, a legend to which we will return in Chapter 8.

Valued in the ancient world for its luminous quality, gold glistens and shines throughout *Electra*: the reward Aegisthus offers to kill Orestes, the gold necklaces and jewellery that Electra would need for the festival, the golden armour and helmet that sets Achilles apart on the battlefield, the magical lamb with its fleece of gold, brought to the gold-wrought temples of Argos.[2] Gold also can introduce a grimmer, darker reality. The 'golden brooches' of Clytemnestra's Trojan slaves glisten against the backdrop of Agamemnon's 'black blood / that rots in the palace' (317–19). On Achilles' gilded sword we see 'the black dust kicked up / by galloping horses' (477–78).[3]

Hair colour matters in Euripides' version of the story. As well as the 'black-fleeced lamb, / its blood recently shed' at Agamemnon's tomb, the Old Man found 'shorn locks of blond hair' (513–15), which he assumes Orestes left as an offering. 'Put the lock of hair up to yours / to see if the colour (*chrôma*) is the same' (520–21), the Old Man tells Electra. It turns out that blond hair runs in the family: Electra accuses her mother of 'sitting before the mirror arranging your long blond tresses' (1071) while Agamemnon was away at war.

It is hardly surprising that Euripides uses colourful language to convey character and mood. But 'non-poetic' diction plays an even more important role in the play. Consider the opening lines of Electra's speech to the corpse of Aegisthus:

> Enough! How shall I start? With the worst,
> or do I save that for last? What words do I fit in between?
> Early every morning I would rehearse everything
> I wanted to say to you straight to your face,
> longing for the day when I would be free from fear.
> Now it has come – time to settle accounts,
> and say all I wanted to say when you were alive.
>
> Eur. *El.* 907–13

A modern version of this scene might show an enraged Electra screaming at her defeated enemy; a contemporary performance artist might splatter the corpse with paint, or pierce her own skin and add her blood to that of the dead man. But Euripides does something different: he has Electra consider the problem of verbal *taksis* ('order'), determining which parts of a speech should go where, with the goal of presenting the most convincing argument. Even though Electra says she has long rehearsed her response to the man she hates, she pauses to consider the most effective rhetorical strategy to make her case against Aegisthus, knowing full well that the dead man will not answer back.[4]

In the climactic scene between mother and daughter, Clytemnestra delivers a powerful defence of her actions, including her murder of Agamemnon. She offers Electra the opportunity to reply, granting her 'freedom to speak' (*parrhêsia*, 1049), the term used in Athens for the free and frank expression guaranteed to citizens in the democratic Assembly. Before responding, Electra says: 'Remember, mother, ... / you gave me liberty to speak my mind' (*parrhêsia*, 1055–56). The repetition emphasizes the importance of speechmaking as a means of self-presentation and as the accepted mode of persuasion in Athenian political life.[5]

As demonstrated in this exchange, Euripides has a tendency to repeat words, sometimes as part of a dialogue, and sometimes to suggest connections between separate parts of the play. To take a small example, the word *skula* ('spoils') occurs three times in *Electra*. Both the Farmer and Clytemnestra refer to the spoils (*skula*) seized by the Greeks after the fall of Troy (6–7, 1000–1). But Orestes uses the word in a very different way, when he presents the corpse of Aegisthus to Electra. He tells her to 'treat him as you like. / Toss him out as scraps for the wild beasts, / or spit him on a stake as spoils (*skulon*) for the birds' (896 –98). If we catch the repetition, we may think of the 'spoils' from Troy more viscerally – the many dead bodies left on the battlefield savaged by wild animals. Or we may appreciate how greatly Orestes' 'conquest' (killing Aegisthus at a sacrifice) differs from his father's victory at Troy, filled with the spoils of war. Or we may feel horror at Orestes' barbaric comparison of impaling a corpse to putting war booty on display, or leaving it out as carrion for vultures.

A more concentrated use of verbal repetition occurs when Clytemnestra prepares to perform the purification rituals after childbirth. She says she will offer the sacrifices as a *charin* (1133) – a 'gift', 'favour', or 'service' – for her daughter's benefit. She then plans to join Aegisthus at his sacrifice to the Nymphs, keen to do her husband that 'service' (*charin*, 1138).[6] After Clytemnestra exits, Electra makes this vow: 'You will become a bride in the house of Hades / to the man you slept with in life. I will do you / this service (*charin*), and you will give me justice for my father' (1144–46). Using the same word three times in thirteen lines, Euripides shifts its meaning from the gift Clytemnestra gives to Electra (performing the ritual), to the 'gift of service' (with sexual overtones) that she owes her husband, and finally to Electra's gift in return, arranging for her mother's union with Aegisthus in the underworld, the just reward for the murder of Agamemnon.

By rough count, Euripides repeats a form of a word within a line or two more than a hundred times in the play.[7] For example, Electra's monody on returning from the spring (112–66) includes the following iterations: 'Walk, I walk' (twice); 'Ah me, poor me' (four times); 'alas, alas' (for her own fate); 'Zeus, Zeus' (invoking his help); 'what city, what home?' (Orestes' exile); 'ah, ah' (before striking her head in grief); 'bitter the axe, bitter the murder plot' (that killed her father). As Electra trudges home with her jug now filled with water, her relentless litany reminds the gods and the elements how much she, her brother, and her dead father have suffered.

At other times, verbal repetition brings out an ironic play on words. Electra informs Orestes (as yet unrecognized), 'I am married (*egêmamesth'*), but a marriage (*gamon*) to death' (247). She accuses her brother of being 'a friend who is absent, not present' (*apôn . . . ou parôn*, 245), with the suggestion that she is 'absent a friend'. Orestes picks up the verbal play on presence and absence when he accepts the Farmer's invitation 'on behalf of your present guest and the non-present son of Agamemnon' (*ho te parôn ho t' ou parôn*, 391). We know that Orestes is both of these characters, but we wonder if he will ever make his true presence known. The double entendre continues when the Old Man recognizes Orestes and joyfully tells Electra to praise the gods. She responds, 'For something absent [that I don't have] or something present [that I do have]?' (*ti tôn apontôn ê ti tôn ontôn peri*, 564). Her question underlines the distance between the man standing before her and the fearless Orestes of her imagination.

Sometimes the repeated words convey the counter-spin of fortune and justice. The Messenger claims that Orestes' murder of Aegisthus returns 'blood for blood' (*haima d' haimatos*, 857). The Chorus agree: 'He did terrible things, and terribly he paid for them' (*epraxe deina, deina d'antedôke*, 957). Electra piles up a similar pattern when she 'prosecutes' Clytemnestra, bringing full circle her mother's claim that Agamemnon's murder was just:

> Why isn't your husband exiled (*antipheugei*) instead of your son
>   (*anti sou posis*)?
> Why hasn't he died instead of me (*out'ant'emou*)? He has killed me (*kteinas*),
> still living, twice as much as my dead sister [Iphigenia]. If murder
> for murder means justice (*phonon dikazôn phonos*), then I will
> kill you (*apoktenô*) myself. / . . . /
> If what you did was just (*dikai'*), then this, too, is just (*endika*).
>   1091–96

Confident that she has found the way to justice, Electra soon learns otherwise. After the matricide, the Chorus share her dismay at what she has done: 'Again and again (*palin palin*) your thoughts (*phronêma*) / change with the wind. / Now you think (*phroneis*) in a purer way, but then / you thought otherwise (*phronousa*), doing a terrible thing / to your unwilling brother' (1201–5). The doubling of words reinforces the to-and-fro nature of murder and regret that sets Euripides' version of the story apart from those of Aeschylus and Sophocles.

The accumulation of verbal echoes also establishes motifs that contribute to the play's overall integrity and dramatic impact. Exile emerges as a major theme, starting with Aegisthus's expulsion of Orestes from Argos and Electra's removal from the palace to the Argive countryside. Electra uses words based on *phuge* ('flight', 'exile') to describe her own situation and that of her brother seven times, and forms of the verb 'wander' (*alateuein*) characterize his unanchored life another five times. Orestes resists murdering Clytemnestra because he fears that matricide will drive him into exile again. After the deed, he realizes he was right: 'What other city can I go to? / What host, what god-fearing man / will dare look on me / since I killed my mother' (1194–97).

Castor confirms Orestes' banishment from his native city: 'You must leave (*eklip'*) Argos behind. It is not for you / to walk the ground of this city, because you killed your mother' (1250–51).[8] Although he will found a new city in Arcadia, separation from his sister and from his ancestral home weighs heavily on Orestes. He bids farewell to Electra: 'robbed of your love, / now I must leave you and be left by you' (*kai s' apoleipsô sou leipomenos*, 1309–10). She, too, must 'leave' (*leipei*, 1312) Argos, although she departs with a new husband. Electra finds this cold comfort, for 'what greater suffering is there / than to leave (*ekleipein*) the borders of your native land?' (1314–15)

Electra's future union with Pylades marks the culmination of another important theme, marriage and its discontents. As noted above, Electra considers her union with the Farmer a 'marriage to death' (247), and in revenge she hopes to make Clytemnestra a 'bride in the house of Hades' (1144), sending her to join Aegisthus in the underworld.[9] The fact that their two corpses lie side by side onstage at the end of the play testifies to Electra's success, but with her mother's blood on her hands she turns the issue back on herself: 'What marriage awaits me? What husband will ever accept me / in his bridal bed?' (1199–1200) Castor provides the answer – Pylades, who was present at the murders of both Aegisthus and Clytemnestra.

Euripides roots the nuptial theme in the experience of his Athenian audience, referring to specific elements of their fifth-century wedding practice. The Farmer mentions the famous 'suitors' (*mnêstêres*, 21) who wished to marry Electra when she came of age, and we learn from

Electra that her cousins Castor and Polydeuces were among those who 'courted' (*emnêsteuon*, 313) her. In ancient Greece, the bride's legal guardian arranged her marriage, setting up a contract (*ekdosis*, 'giving away') with the groom. Electra explains that the Farmer 'was not the man to whom my father expected to give me away' (*ekdôsein*, 249). Her husband never consummated the marriage because he knew Aegisthus had no right to 'give me away' (*donta*, 259; also *dous*, 267). That authority lay with her brother Orestes, as her closest living male relative. Castor restores this proper relationship at the end of the play, telling Orestes to 'give away (*dos*) Electra to Pylades to take home as his wife' (1249).

Speaking to her daughter, Clytemnestra describes her own betrothal: 'My father Tyndareus did not give me away (*edôke*) to your father / so that I or the children I bore would be killed' (1018–19). By pretending he had arranged their daughter's marriage to Achilles, Agamemnon lured Iphigenia to Aulis, where he sacrificed her so the ships could sail to Troy.[10] Ten years later, Agamemnon returned from the war with the prophetess Cassandra, 'installing her in our bed / so that now there were two brides in the same house' (1033–34). In defiance, Clytemnestra acquires a new man, Aegisthus, whom she weds after they join forces to murder Agamemnon.

Electra calls this second marriage shameful and unholy, for Clytemnestra won her 'deceitful bedmate / ... / with a two-edged sword' (164–66). From that time on, the murderous couple 'sleep together / in a bloodstained nuptial bed' (211–12). Although he is dead, Electra berates Aegisthus for marrying Clytemnestra: 'You went so far in your folly to think / that after you married my mother, she would stay true, / even though she adulterated the bed of my father' (918–20). Clytemnestra levels a similar charge at Menelaus for 'marrying that whore Helen, / a wife he did not know how to control, / and one who betrayed him' (1027–29).

Weddings and marital life play a particularly pernicious role in the house of Atreus, infamous for the troubled unions of Thyestes and Aerope, Aerope and Atreus, Menelaus and Helen, Agamemnon and Clytemnestra, and Clytemnestra and Aegisthus. Euripides implicitly contrasts their various sexual infidelities with the marriage of Electra and the Farmer, where sex plays no role. The mythic background (and Euripides' addition to it) adds a double edge to the Chorus's opinion on the subject: 'With regard to women and marriage, chance holds the cards. / Some mortals have good luck; others do not' (1100–1).

A more public motif running through *Electra* centres around athletic competition, an important aspect of ancient Greek life. Panhellenic ('all-Greek') athletic festivals took place at Nemea, Isthmia, Olympia, and Delphi, and all but the first are mentioned in the play.[11] The victors in each event won a garland – made of olive leaves at Olympia, pine at Isthmia, wild celery at Nemea, and laurel at the Pythian games in Delphi. On their return to their home cities, winning athletes were lauded with the choral performance of a victory ode (*epinikia*) commissioned in their honour.[12]

References to athletics occur in almost all Greek tragedies, but they carry a particular relevance in those dealing with the house of Atreus. The father of Atreus and grandfather of Agamemnon was Pelops, who won a fateful chariot race to win his wife and kingdom. King Oenomaus set this competitive test for any suitor of his daughter Hippodamia – victory in a chariot race against himself, or death. The decapitated heads of eighteen contenders for his daughter's hand, mounted on the columns of his palace, provided fair warning.[13] Pelops bribed Oenomaus's charioteer to tamper with the royal chariot, causing it to crash and kill the king.[14] Winning the race and the princess, Pelops became the new ruler and founded the Olympic games in honour of his triumph. However, as punishment for his deceit, he suffered a deadly curse on his descendants.

Although never referring directly to Pelops, Euripides weaves aspects of the story into *Electra*, applying racing and other athletic vocabulary to important dramatic moments. As noted above, Aegisthus holds his fatal sacrifice in the 'the fields where he pastures his horses' (623). Orestes and Pylades pretend to be athletes from Thessaly on their way to the Olympic games (781–82), and Aegisthus invites them to join the proceedings, noting the talent of Thessalians for breaking horses (815–17).[15] We recall Electra's less flattering view of horse-loving Aegisthus, when she reviles him for 'mounting my father's chariot, and parading up and down' (320), insulting Agamemnon's memory by brandishing his sceptre as if it belonged to him.

Horses, chariots, and the Olympic games come together in an associative nexus with other sports.[16] At Aegisthus's invitation, Orestes flays the bull-calf 'faster / than a runner could finish both legs of a hippodrome course' (824 –25). When Orestes brings Aegisthus's corpse back to his sister, she praises him 'not for winning some pointless foot race / but for having killed our enemy' (883–84). Mocking the dead Aegisthus, Electra observes that a criminal may think he's got a head start, but he'd be wrong to think he has beaten justice 'until he crosses the finish line / and completes life's final lap' (955–56). Uncertain how Electra's childbirth scheme will unfold, the Old Man impatiently tells her to 'get past the turning post and bring us to last lap of your plot' (659). Castor reminds Orestes that he must 'run the full distance of a trial for murder' (1264). Combative sports also enter the play, when Electra refers to Orestes' training in a wrestling school (528) and imagines his encounter with Aegisthus as a culminating match: 'If, outwrestled, you take a deadly fall, / I too will die' (686–87).

Orestes boasts that he has come to 'win the victor's crown' (*stephanon*, 614); after he slays Aegisthus, the palace slaves 'crown his head' (*stephousi … kara*, 854) and celebrate. Arriving with the news of Orestes' success, the Messenger addresses the Chorus: 'O Mycenaean maidens, glorious in victory' (*kallinikoi*, 761). The term *kallinikos*, 'beautiful/glorious victor', occurs regularly in epinician odes that celebrate victorious athletes, and the Chorus perform just such a song in praise of Orestes: 'He has won the victor's crown (*nikai stephanaphorian*) / greater than those won by the banks of the Alpheus' (862–63; the Alpheus river runs through Olympia).[17] The maidens continue their 'song of glorious victory' (*kallinikon*, 865), and Electra promises to 'crown (*stepsô*) the head of my brother who brings victory home (*nikêphorou*)' (872).

When Orestes enters, Electra continues where the Chorus left off: 'O glorious victor (*kallinike*), born of a father / who brought victory home (*nikêphoron*) from Troy, / Orestes, accept this garland for the tresses of your hair' (880–82). She offers a similar crown to his loyal comrade: 'Accept from my hand / this garland (*stephanon*), Pylades, / for you win a prize equal to his / in this contest' (887–89). The language of athletic triumph and joyful homecoming sounds like verbal overkill, as if to camouflage the fact that the 'contest' Orestes and Pylades won involved a brutal murder. Lest we forget the bloodshed, Euripides has the victors return with the body of Aegisthus, whose gruesome death the Messenger described only fifty lines before.

Blood and gore are no strangers to Greek tragedy, but its verbal presence in *Electra* merits our attention, providing a counterpoint to the 'poetic colouring' with which this chapter began. Ancient Greek has many ways to indicate violent death, and Euripides employs most of them in the play: *kteinô*, meaning simply 'to kill'; *thuô*, 'to sacrifice' (usually used of a ritual offering, *thusia*, of an animal to the gods); *sphazô*, 'to slay or slaughter' (with sacrificial undertones, linked to *sphagis*, a 'sacrificial knife'); and *phoneuô*, 'to murder' (linked to *phonê*, 'bloodshed'). Forms of the generic verb 'to kill', *kteinô*, occur over thirty times in *Electra*: Agamemnon kills Priam at Troy; Aegisthus kills Agamemnon and wants to kill Orestes; Orestes kills Aegisthus; Agamemnon kills Iphigenia; Clytemnestra kills her husband; Orestes kills Clytemnestra; and Ares kills Halirrhothius, which leads to the foundation of the homicide court in Athens.

Although this litany seems distressing enough, Euripides darkens his vocabulary in various ways. We see this in his depiction of animal sacrifice – referred to often in the play – the *sine qua non* of ancient Greek religion. Euripides uses the standard term for sacrifice, *thuô*, for the ritual offerings at the Argive Heraion, Aegisthus's sacrifice to the Nymphs, the offerings that Orestes makes to Olympian Zeus, and the sacrifice Clytemnestra will undertake as purification rites after the birth of Electra's child. As soon as Clytemnestra enters the cottage to perform the ritual, however, Electra applies the language of animal sacrifice to her mother: 'You will offer up (*thuseis*) the kind of sacrifice (*thuê*) that is fitting to the gods' (1141).

Tragedians often blur the distinction between animal sacrifice and human murder,[18] but Euripides is second to none in conveying the visceral details. The Messenger's account of Aegisthus's murder (discussed in Chapter 3) begins with a point-by-point description of an animal sacrifice, including preparation, death, flaying, and disembowelment. Here Euripides prefers words related to *sphazô*, 'to sacrifice' with a sense of the 'slaughter' involved in the act. Aegisthus will 'slaughter a bullock' (*bousphagein*, 627) for the Nymphs, using a 'sacrificial knife' (*sphagida*, 811) to 'slit its throat' (*k'asphax'*, 813), and then catching the blood in the 'ritual bowl' (*sphageion*, 800). Orestes uses similar language for his offering of a lamb at Agamemnon's tomb (*epesphaks'*, 92), and the Old Man sees evidence of this recent 'sacrifice with shed blood (*sphagion ... haima*) on the ground' (514).

Accustomed to this ritual practice, the Greek audience would have felt nothing odd or disturbing in these accounts of animal sacrifice. However, they may have raised an eyebrow when Electra laments the 'slaughter' (*sphagais*, 124) of Agamemnon and mourns him as a 'slain [sacrificial] victim' (*sphagiasmôn*, 200). Or when she plans to 'shed the blood' (*haim' episphaxas'*, 281) of her mother, using a 'sacrificial knife' (*sphagis*, 1142). Threatening suicide if Orestes fails, Electra readies her own 'slaughter' (*sphagên*, 757) but stops when her brother returns in triumph with Aegisthus's corpse, which they must hide from the woman they plan to 'butcher' (*sphagês*, 961). After Clytemnestra's murder, Electra and Orestes cover up the 'wounds' (*sphagas*, 1228) they have inflicted on her body, the signs of 'slaughter' (*sphagas*, 1243) that draw the Dioskouroi to Argos. Castor insists that neither brother nor sister are 'polluted with this [sacrificial] bloodshed' (*sphagiois*, 1294), although they must go into exile. Time and again, Euripides depicts the murders of Agamemnon, Aegisthus, and Clytemnestra in terms of a (perverted) sacrifice.

As we might expect, the normal word for 'blood' – *haima* – appears frequently in *Electra*, but Euripides prefers the word *phonos* ('murder', 'bloodshed', 'bloody') which occurs in various forms some forty times in the play. Clytemnestra luxuriates 'in her bloodstained bed' (*lektrois phoniois*, 211), and Aegisthus brandishes in his 'bloodstained hands' (*miaiphonoisi chersi*, 322) the sceptre of the king he killed. The Chorus hope to see Clytemnestra's 'dark blood (*phonion* ... *haima*) pouring / from her neck, sliced by the sword' (485–86). Orestes will pay back his 'father's murders with more murder' (*phonon* ... *phoneusi*, 89), a sentiment echoed by Electra who claims that 'murder for murder' (*phonon* ... *phonos*, 1094) makes for a just exchange. When Zeus sends a phantom of Helen to Troy, he does so to promote human 'carnage' (*phonos*, 1282).

Euripides uses several other words for bloodshed, but the ones we have looked at make the point. *Electra* overflows with the language of killing, bloodletting, sacrifice, butchery, slaughter, murder. On average, a word evoking the deed or its result occurs every ten lines. Although we see Clytemnestra walking to her death, and corpses appear onstage more than once, the violence and bloodshed in the play depend primarily on Euripides' language to focus the audience's imagination.

In contrast to the accumulation of words and images linked to bloodletting, *Electra* includes a range of aphoristic and proverbial utterances dealing with day-to-day life. The Farmer confesses that 'nobility is not worth much / without money to back it up' (37–38). He says that those who second-guess his chastity 'measure modesty / in a crooked scale' (52–53). As a working man, he knows that 'words to the gods can fill your mouth / but it's work that fills your stomach' (80–81). He claims that 'any woman worth her salt / can find something in the pantry' (422–23), while admitting that 'money helps when you need it' (427). Even so, he takes comfort in the fact that 'rich or poor, / a man can only eat so much' (430–31).

Aphorisms are not limited to the Farmer. Orestes thinks that 'too much wisdom / can lead to folly' (295–96). He knows from experience that 'exiles are powerless' (236), a phrase that his sister repeats verbatim (352). Electra enjoys 'the pleasure that comes from too many tears' (126). She believes that 'a man who marries above his station / is trumped by his wife' (936–37), and that 'ill-gotten gains profit little, / but a noble nature lasts a lifetime' (940–41). In her view, 'the wife who flaunts her beauty / is looking for trouble' (1074–75). Taunting her mother, Electra claims that 'bad behavior sets the standard for good / and makes it shine even brighter' (1084–85).

When Clytemnestra wonders why her daughter could find no midwife to help, Electra reminds her that 'poverty has no friends' (1131). The Old Man shares the same observation with Orestes, having learned that 'No one loves you when you're down and out' (literally, 'no one befriends you in misfortune'). He adds that 'a friend in need is a friend indeed' (literally, 'what a find / when someone shares both good and bad with you', 605–7). The Chorus utter their own bit of proverbial wisdom that supports a patriarchal view of marriage: 'A wife should give way to her husband in all things' (1052). At the end of the play, we may wonder if things will work out that way for Pylades, who takes Electra home as his new wife.

Explaining why Electra and Orestes can never return to their homeland, Castor concludes gnomically, 'common deeds make for a common fate' (1305).[19] That may be true, but it leaves unanswered the moral questions around murder, matricide, and the purposeless bloodshed of the Trojan War. The platitudes and aphorisms remind us that for all its mythic pedigree, *Electra* keeps its feet on the ground, and asks its readers and audience to do the same. Language provides that common ground, and close attention to the words is crucial for our understanding of how the play works, and what it is working towards.

Setting, Costumes, Props and Bodies

As we have seen, *Electra* depends on a rich mixture of language – rhetorical, poetic, imagistic, descriptive, proverbial. Like all live theatre, Greek tragedy also had an essential *material* aspect: the physical space where the performance took place (the theatre of Dionysus in Athens, discussed in Chapter 1); the setting for each tragedy; the actors whose costumes, gestures, and movement helped bring their characters to life; and the props they used to tell the story.

Electra takes place on a rural farm in the Argive countryside, understood as overlooking the Inachus river valley, isolated, atop a steep hill. The hut is described as dirty, shack-like, with soot-covered walls, lacking a well-stocked larder. Perhaps the set decoration made some of this visible, but the performance schedule at the City Dionysia prohibited complicated set changes.[1] As a result, we cannot tell how literally or realistically the scenic backdrop suggested the play's setting. Euripides takes great pains to establish the rural location of the play through verbal description, and also through the physicality of the actors.

Shortly before dawn, the Farmer prepares for his morning labours, including spring ploughing with his oxen. A stream flows nearby, where Electra goes to fetch water with her jug. The house seems remote, albeit within walking distance of Agamemnon's tomb, the Tutor's dwelling near the Tanaus river and Spartan territory, and the horse pastures where Aegisthus holds his sacrifice to the Nymphs.[2] Now a shepherd, the old Tutor complains of the difficult ascent to the cottage, bent over double, his legs tottering. Electra earlier refers to her 'exile on this mountain crag' (*El.* 210), indicating its steep isolation.

Reflecting the environment of the play, characters emphasize movement, walking, taking steps (often difficult ones) towards a destination.³ On her return from the stream, Electra issues a set of self-exhortations: 'Hasten your step, walk, keep moving' (112–13, 127–28). At the sight of strange men, she tells the Chorus 'Flee down the track, and I'll run to the house / and we'll escape these criminals on foot' (218–19). Orestes races from his hiding place to cut his sister off.⁴ The Old Man tries to prove to Electra that her brother has returned, telling her to visit Agamemnon's tomb and 'step into his footprint, and see whether the tread of his boot / aligns with your foot' (532 –33). When the two strangers emerge from the cottage to meet the Old Man, they 'step out with nimble feet' (549),⁵ eager to return to the open air. That eagerness fades when Agamemnon's Tutor begins to scrutinize Orestes, and the young man asks with trepidation, 'Why are his feet circling around me?' (561).

Following the long-delayed recognition scene, Orestes and his party leave to kill Aegisthus, their journey described by the Messenger: 'After we took our feet from this dwelling, stepping / onto a wagon track wide enough for two carts, / we made our way to where the new lord of Mycenae / happened to be standing in a well-watered garden' (774–77). At the end of the play, departure from Argos involves everyone but the Chorus. Castor reminds Orestes that 'there is no city / you can walk in' (1250–1) until 'you move your feet ... / and make your way' to Athens (1288–89). On the way, 'the Furies will track you, their footsteps like terror' (1344). The Farmer, too, must abandon his land and cottage, for Pylades and Electra will take him to their new home in Phocis. After the Chorus exit (customary at the end of a tragic performance), only the dead bodies of Aegisthus and Clytemnestra remain.

References to bodily exertion, manual labour, and physical contact help create the sense of a rural world. The word for hand (*cheir*) is uttered over twenty-five times in the play, and Euripides often calls attention to his characters' handiwork: Electra carries her jug of water; the Tutor arrives with an armful of food;⁶ Orestes' party returns with Aegisthus's corpse; they later take it into the cottage to hide it from Clytemnestra; Electra crowns her brother and Pylades with garlands, and she offers Clytemnestra her hand when she steps down from the wagon.[7] Appealing to her unnamed guest, Electra merges language with her own body: 'Take this message to Orestes: / ... the voices are many: / my hands, my tongue, my broken heart, / my razor-slashed hair ...' (332 –35).[8] Mirroring the embrace that brings their recognition scene to a close, Electra and Orestes cling to one another at the end of the play, their final contact before separation and exile.

Moving from bodies and their gestural life to costume, *Electra* explores the problem we all experience trying to 'read' other people by what they show of themselves on the surface. On first seeing his sister, Orestes mistakes her for a slave girl, completely misled by her appearance. Complaining that she lacks proper attire, Electra refuses to attend the festival of Hera, but she rejects the Chorus's offer to lend her a dress and jewellery.[9] She explains to the stranger, 'Stabled in these clothes / and covered with dirt, / ... / I must make the garments myself, toiling at the loom, / or else go naked' (304–8).[10] When the Old Tutor wipes his tears on his own 'tattered robes' (501), Electra wonders if he weeps at her own appearance.[11] On seeing her daughter, Clytemnestra comments on how 'unwashed and poorly clothed' (1107) she looks after giving birth.

At the other end of the spectrum, Orestes declares that Clytemnestra 'shines with finery' (966) when she approaches the cottage, accompanied by her Trojan slaves.[12] With chilling irony Electra warns her mother to take care on entering the cottage, lest 'the sooty walls stain your dress' (*peplous*, 1140), the same dress (*peplôn*, 1206) that Clytemnestra rips open when she begs her children for mercy. The difference between robes and rags, between clean garments and filthy ones, ceases to matter when both are covered with blood.

Orestes' costume also draws the attention of others. Returning from the fields, the Farmer thinks that the strange men talking to his wife must be city-folk, an indication that Orestes and Pylades are dressed distinctively. The Tutor concludes the same thing when he first sees the young men – 'They appear to be gentlemen (*eugeneis*, literally "well-born"), but they could prove counterfeit' (550). We know Orestes has returned in disguise, and his clothing – while revealing his status – helps to mask his true identity.

In order to infiltrate Aegisthus's banquet, Orestes and Pylades pretend to be Thessalian athletes heading for the Olympic games. Asked by his host to flay the sacrificed bull, Orestes removes the 'gorgeous cloak' (820) from his shoulders and gets down to work. This presumably is the same 'cloak that he draws' (*epibalôn pharê*, 1221) over his eyes when he kills Clytemnestra, and that he and Electra use to 'draw over' (*pharea tad' amphiballomen*, 1231) their mother's corpse after the murder.[13] Operating as visual shorthand, Orestes' costume helps us track his transformation from cautious prevaricator to bloodstained matricide.

'Wreaths' or 'garlands' (*stephanoi*) serve as a significant stage prop in the play. Clytemnestra did not welcome home the triumphant Agamemnon with 'victory garlands' (*stephanois*, 163), but Orestes returns to Argos in the hope of gaining a 'victor's wreath' (*stephanos*, 614) when he kills his father's murderers. Actual garlands come into play with the arrival of the Tutor, who brings 'festive wreaths' (*stephanous*, 496) along with food and wine to welcome the guests. But the recognition of Orestes intervenes, and no meal eventuates. One might say that Aegisthus's feast takes its place, for Orestes and his party find the tyrant 'plucking tender myrtle leaves as a woven garland for his head' (778), part of the festivities he invites the strangers to join.[14]

After Aegisthus's murder, the Messenger describes how the older slaves recognize Orestes and 'crown his head with garlands' (*stephousi . . . kara*, 854), anticipating the onstage ceremony that Electra prepares for her brother and Pylades, discussed in Chapter 5. When Orestes returns after his triumph, he may still be wearing the garlands he received after the murder. Would Electra remove them before garlanding her brother a second time? Or was Orestes 'double-crowned', a kind of visual overkill that mocks the ostensible glory of his triumph?[15]

Unlike ceremonies for athletic victors, the celebration of Orestes' triumph includes the losers as well as the winners, for he and his crew bring Aegisthus's corpse back with them. Electra's epinician praise for the victors then gives way to its rhetorical opposite, her malediction directed at a fatally defeated opponent.[16] The ritual garlands worn by all three men – remember that Aegisthus wreathed his head with myrtle fronds for the banquet – conjoin athletic victory and bloodshed, heroic celebration and insults over a corpse.

Stage props tend towards the minimal in Greek tragedy, although they can prove essential to the plot, as we find in Sophocles' *Philoctetes* (the bow), his *Electra* (Orestes' funeral urn), and his *Women of Trachis* (the poisoned robe). Props of a more mundane nature appear in Euripides' *Electra*, perhaps more of them than in any other tragedy. As noted above, almost every character brings something on when making their entrance – a jug, a sword, food and drink, a corpse. When Electra returns with water from the spring, she tells herself to put the jug down so she can better lament her dead father. The day-to-day realities of farm life literally get in the way of the heroic suffering to which she aspires.

When the old Tutor arrives from his farm, he brings food and supplies and the aforementioned garlands: cheese, wine (in a wine skin,

Fig. 4 Elektra (Irene Pappas) and Chorus, from *Elektra* (1962), directed by Michael Cacoyannis. Courtesy of the Michael Cacoyannis Foundation.

indicated at 511), and a lamb. In no other tragedy does an animal specifically meant for food appear on stage. The presence of a lamb – as well as wine and cheese – seems more at home in a comedy of Aristophanes.[17] However, Euripides cleverly weaves sheep and lambs into the fabric of the drama. The Tutor describes the remains of a black lamb sacrificed at Agamemnon's tomb, evidence of Orestes' return. Euripides then introduces a *magical* lamb into the story when the Chorus sing of the golden lamb stolen by Thyestes. Possessing this animal prodigy enables him to seize power from his brother Atreus, an event of such gravity that the gods change the course of the sun. The onstage presence of the Tutor's lamb – meant to be slaughtered and eaten, but forgotten in the rush to murder – sets the table for the Chorus's lyric evocation of the magic lamb of myth.[18]

In the original production at the City Dionysia, Clytemnestra entered the orchestra (along with her attendants and Trojan slaves) on a horse-drawn wagon. Aegisthus holds his feast for the Nymphs in the meadows where he pastures horses, and Clytemnestra plans to travel to meet him after she helps Electra. Earlier the Chorus sing of the horses engraved on Achilles' sword hilt, kicking up dust as they race by, evoking the dragging of Hector's corpse around the walls of Troy. With Clytemnestra's arrival, the ancient audience saw live horses bringing the Queen to her death.[19] In her last onstage act, Clytemnestra instructs her slaves to take the horses out to graze and return when she has completed the birth ritual (1135–36). Euripides' audience watched the horses and wagon led out of the theatre, to wait in vain for their regal passenger.

One other stage prop demands our attention – Orestes' sword. We know he arrives on stage armed, for Electra indicates as much when she flees from him: 'Why, with sword drawn, were you waiting in ambush near my house?' (225). We presume Orestes used the weapon to sacrifice the sheep at his father's grave (92), and that he plans to kill Aegisthus with it. However, Euripides surprises us with some cleverly dramatic 'misdirection'. In place of the sword, Aegisthus gives his new guest a 'well-hammered Doric knife' (819) to display his skill, and Orestes flays the sacrificed calf with panache, leading us to believe he then will use the knife as the murder weapon. But Orestes asks for 'a Phthian cleaver instead of this Doric blade' (836) to split the beast's breastbone, which he does, and then uses the same butcher's tool to smash Aegisthus's backbone.[20] Only after the murder do Orestes and Pylades draw their swords to protect themselves, until someone recognizes Agamemnon's son, and jubilation replaces confrontation.

In terms of shedding human blood, Euripides saves Orestes' sword for Clytemnestra. At first his mother's desperate plea stops Orestes in his tracks: 'My hands had to drop the weapon' (1217). But he steels himself, covering his eyes with his cloak, and then 'I sacrificed my mother, / driving my sword into her neck' (1222–23). The prop we have seen from Orestes' first entrance finally does what it was meant to do. But by this time, he – and many in the audience – wishes his sword had not fulfilled its 'destiny'.

Although not normally considered props, two corpses appear on stage, those of Aegisthus and Clytemnestra. We don't know how the ancient theatre represented a corpse, but the tragedians probably used a dummy or a mute actor, dressed in the costume and mask of the character who had been killed. Because Aegisthus never appears alive onstage, the look of his corpse (if any features were visible) was not pre-determined. As noted above, the servants of Orestes and Pylades bring what's left of Aegisthus into the theatre via an *eisodos*. The arrival of a body from offstage occurs frequently in tragedy, usually followed by a mourning scene over the dead. Only in Euripides' *Electra* is a corpse brought onstage from outside the theatre (i.e. not displayed on the *ekkuklêma*) for the specific purpose of abusing it. Orestes encourages his sister 'to outrage the corpse' (*nekrous hubrizen*, 902), exposing it to the ravages of dogs and birds.[21] Following Electra's diatribe, Orestes orders the body removed to the cottage in order to hide it from their mother. After the matricide, the corpse appears once again, this time on the *ekkuklêma* with that of Clytemnestra.[22]

The Messenger announces to Electra that her brother 'comes / to show you something, not the head (*kara*) of the Gorgon, / but Aegisthus, whom you hate' (855–57). These lines refer to Perseus's beheading of the gorgon Medusa, one of the foundation myths of the city of Argos. With that story in mind, many scholars believe that Orestes has decapitated Aegisthus, bringing both the head and the corpse onstage.[23] The idea that Electra addresses much of her speech to Aegisthus's head (however it was represented) brings together several elements in the play that otherwise seem puzzling, and does so to great dramatic effect.

To understand why this scenario makes sense, we need to look briefly at the Perseus myth. When an oracle informs Acrisius, an early king of Argos, that his daughter Danae will bear a son who will kill him, Acrisius locks her up in a bronze chamber (open to the sky so she can breathe) to ensure she never has a child. Enamoured of her beauty, Zeus impregnates Danae with a shower of gold from above, and she gives birth to Perseus. Once he has grown, Perseus is sent on an impossible mission to kill the gorgon Medusa, who turns to stone anyone whose gaze meets hers.[24] With the help of Athena and Hermes, and the use of either a mirror or reflective shield to avoid direct eye contact, Perseus decapitates Medusa. In thanks for the goddess's assistance, he gives the head to Athena, who incorporates it as an apotropaic device on her goat-haired breastplate (or shield) known as the *aegis.* At the moment of her decapitation, Medusa's blood spontaneously generates a winged horse (Pegasus), which the hero Bellerophon rides in his quest to kill another monster, the tri-formed Chimaera, who has a lion's head, the body of a goat, and serpent's tail.

The story found its way into many tragedies, all of them lost. Aeschylus produced a tetralogy on the Perseus myth; Sophocles' wrote three plays based on the legend; Euripides' *Danae* deals with her impregnation, and his *Dictys* seems to have dealt with Danae's fate when Perseus leaves to pursue the gorgon.[25] Sophocles and Euripides each wrote an *Andromeda,* dealing with Perseus's post-gorgon adventure in which he saves the Ethiopian princess Andromeda from a sea-monster.[26] Both of these plays seem to have culminated in the conversion into constellations of Perseus, Andromeda, her father Cepheus, her mother Cassiopeia, and the sea-monster Cetus, much like the transformation of Castor and Polydeuces into the twin stars of Gemini.

References to Perseus and his story occur throughout *Electra*.[27] In the first *stasimon* he is on the rim of Achilles' shield, holding 'the head of the Gorgon' (*El.* 460). The Chorus describe Achilles' breastplate, which depicts the Chimaera fleeing Bellerophon, who rides on 'the winged horse Pegasus' (475), born from the blood that flowed from Medusa's severed head. Following the matricide, Orestes wonders 'Who ... / will dare look on my face' (*kara*, literally 'head', 1195–96), as if he had become gorgon-like himself.[28] Orestes had to cover his eyes before driving his sword through his mother's neck (1221–23), reminding us again of the beheading of Medusa. Just as she earlier helped Perseus, Athena will protect Orestes from the Furies by holding her gorgon shield (the aforementioned *aegis*) over his head (*kara*, 1257). The presence of so many strands of the Perseus myth supports the view that Orestes has decapitated Aegisthus.

Other Greek tragedies refer to the beheading and dismemberment of corpses. The Egyptian herald threatens to cut off the Danaids' heads in Aeschylus's *Suppliant Women* (836–40).[29] Assailing the Furies in *Eumenides*, Apollo claims they only belong where decapitation and mutilation serve as punishment (A. *Eum.* 186–90). In Sophocles' *Ajax*, Tecmessa describes how Ajax mutilated livestock and decapitated a ram; later the deranged hero appears on the *ekkuklêma* surrounded by the bloody carcasses (S. *Aj.* 235–44, 346–47).

Euripides specializes in this kind of brutality: in *Hecuba* the blinded Polymnestor wants to tear the Trojan Queen to pieces and gorge on her flesh (Eur. *Hec.* 1070–74); the one-eyed protagonist dashes out the brains of one of Odysseus's crew in the satyr play *Cyclops* (400–4); swinging his mace against the Thebans, Theseus 'snaps off necks, / harvesting a crop of helmeted heads' in *Suppliant Women* (*Supp.* 716–17); the protagonist in *Heracles* vows to decapitate the tyrant Lycus and throw his head to the dogs (Eur. *HF* 567–68). This method of execution also recalls the story of Pelops, discussed in Chapter 5, where Oenomaus affixed the heads of the defeated suitors to the columns in his palace.

The most famous beheading in tragedy occurs in Euripides' *Bacchae*. The Theban king Pentheus threatens to decapitate the Lydian stranger

(Eur. *Ba.* 241), and then suffers that punishment himself (1125–43). His mother Agave returns from the mountain with the impaled head of her son, represented by the mask worn by the actor who played Pentheus – the very actor who now plays his mother.[30] Agave thinks she holds the head of a lion, until her father brings her to her senses, and together they try to arrange the scattered bits of Pentheus for burial (Eur. *Ba* 1168–1300). The beheading of Aegisthus's corpse in *Electra* lies well within Euripides' repertoire.

Aegisthus's decapitation offers clear advantages for staging the scene in the theatre of Dionysus. Unlike most monologues in tragedy, Electra's tirade is aimed at the face of the man she hates: 'I never stopped rehearsing what I wanted to say to your face' (*kat' omma son*, literally 'into your eyes', *El.* 910).[31] Assailing him as seducer of her mother and murderer of her father, Electra directs her venom at Aegisthus's

Fig. 5 Electra (Roxanne Hart) with the head of Aegisthus, Chorus members, from the 1973 Theatre Intime production of *Electra*, translated and directed by Rush Rehm. Photograph: John Coventry.

appearance: 'You, with your good looks! But I prefer a husband / who doesn't have girlish features, but looks like a man' (948–49).[32] Although tragic acting was not realistic in our sense of the term, we can imagine the difficulty for the actor in a large, open-air theatre, with most of the audience sitting above him, having to speak to Aegisthus's corpse as it lies on the ground. It would be far more effective to have a graspable object for Electra to address, much as Agave holds the mask ('head') of her son in *Bacchae*.

Throughout *Electra*, Euripides calls attention to a character's face, neck, hair, and head. When the Messenger returns to the stage, he expresses surprise that Electra does not recognize his face (*prosôpou*, 768) from before, when he appeared as a (silent) servant of Orestes. For her part, Electra accuses her mother of tarting herself up for other men, 'showing your prettified / face (*prosôpon*) in public' (1074–75).[33] The Chorus imagine Clytemnestra's death: 'One day I will see the bloody gore below her neck / pouring down to the ground from the sword's blow' (485–86). The actual murder takes this form, for Orestes drives his sword through his mother's neck (1222–23). The garlanding of Orestes, Pylades, and Aegisthus directs attention to the crown of the head (*kara*, 778, 854; *krata*, 872, 874) and the hair (*komês*, 870–71, 882). Electra threatens to commit suicide by striking her head (*kara*, 688) with a sword if her brother fails to kill Aegisthus.[34] Time and again Electra talks about her hair, razor-cropped and filthy, in contrast to Clytemnestra's groomed, blond tresses. Orestes leaves a lock of his hair at Agamemnon's tomb, which the Tutor unsuccessfully hopes to match with Electra's. The snake-haired monster Medusa, whom Perseus decapitates, fits into this scenario, indirectly supporting the view that Electra addresses the head of her hated nemesis.

Unlike the face of Medusa that petrifies the onlooker, that of Aegisthus provides a focal point for Electra to direct her anger. After speaking to Aegisthus's head, she might return it to the corpse with her dismissive 'To hell with you' (literally, 'Away with you', 952). Her closing lines bring us back to images of movement, footwork, and physical exertion with which we began this chapter: 'Let no criminal think that because he runs / his first steps in the race well, he can gain / a victory over Justice. Wait till he reaches / the finish line . . .' (953–56). Addressed to a man whose backbone has been smashed, Electra's vision of Aegisthus reaching a finish line seems bizarre in the extreme.

We have examined the attention that Euripides pays to important visible and physical aspects of his story, interweaving setting, props, costumes, and the performers' bodies with the language of the play. In the next chapter, we will explore a set of related themes arising from this combination, focusing on the representation of gender and sex, children and childbirth.

Gender, Sex and Reproductive Roles

Maleness, Mothers and Offspring

In his prologue, the Farmer informs the audience that the murdered Agamemnon left behind 'a male (*arsena*) and female (*thêlu*) shoot' (*El.* 15), namely Orestes and Electra.[1] By highlighting the gender differences, the Farmer introduces an important theme that runs through the play. As Agamemnon's son, Orestes is the legitimate ruler in Argos and the likely avenger of his father's murder. He poses an immediate threat to Aegisthus and Clytemnestra. Electra, on the other hand, presents a longer-term problem – as Agamemnon's daughter, she one day might bear male offspring who would inherit the throne, should her brother perish. Once Electra is married off to the Farmer, that problem vanishes.[2]

The ancient Greeks viewed marriage as the fulfilment to which all girls aspire, assuming the roles of bride, wife, and mother.[3] Tragedy offers many examples of doomed ingénues lamenting the fact that they will die unmarried: the title characters in Sophocles' *Antigone* (810–15), and in Euripides' *Iphigenia in Aulis* (1343, 1399) and *Iphigenia among the Taurians* (856–58); Electra and Chrysothemis in Sophocles' *Electra* (187–90); Polyxena in Euripides' *Hecuba* (416) and Macaria in *Children of Heracles* (579–80). Mothers and fathers in tragedy worry about the marital prospects of their daughters. The blind Oedipus asks Creon to oversee his young daughters' future marriages near the end of Sophocles' *Oedipus Tyrannus* (1492–1510). As the guardian of his sister Antigone, Eteocles re-affirms her betrothal to Haimon in Euripides' *Phoenician Women* (757–60), and Helen expresses dismay that Hermione remains unwedded back in Sparta in *Helen* (283–84, 688–90, 933).

In *Electra*, Euripides works a perverse variation on concerns over an unmarried daughter. The marriage arranged for Electra represents the opposite of a good match, but it serves Aegisthus and Clytemnestra's purposes. Unbeknownst to them, Electra's husband respects his wife's royal lineage, and she remains a virgin. Even if that arrangement were to change, any offspring that might result would not threaten Aegisthus's rule.

In spite of the unorthodox nature of their union, Electra and the Farmer adopt surprisingly conventional gender roles, but with the occasional twist one associates with domestic comedy. After complaining to the heavens of the demeaning menial labour forced upon her, Electra rejects her husband's offer to help and insists that she's keen to be a good wife and take care of the household chores. When he sees Electra talking to strange men, the Farmer suspects impropriety, a sign of his traditional social values. He quickly reverses himself when he learns that the strangers come from Orestes, and he invites them into his poor cottage. His generosity angers Electra, who berates him for forgetting the superior status of their visitors. The Farmer asserts a last vestige of male authority, telling Electra to find something for the guests to eat. He then follows her orders and leaves to get the old shepherd, who can provide decent provisions. Gender roles flip back and forth, in humorous, and sometimes unsettling, ways.

While acknowledging her husband's kindness to her, Electra has no doubt about what constitutes real virility and male courage, especially as it concerns her brother. She chastises the Old Man for implying that Orestes might return in secret, out of fear. She wonders how he could think that the hair of her brother, raised in the manly environment of wrestling schools, could resemble her own, all combed and 'feminine' (*thêlus*, 529), the same word used by the Farmer in the prologue. When the Old Man suggests that her footprint might resemble the one left at Agamemnon's tomb, Electra reminds him that 'the feet of siblings are not equal, when one is a boy (*andros*) / and the other a girl (*gunaikos*): the male (*arsên*) is larger' (536–37). We may find nothing peculiar in Electra's emphasis on how genders differ, but the fact that she returns to the subject in her speech to Aegisthus's corpse suggests that more is going on.[4]

Electra disparages the dead man for not being a *bona fide* male, and extends her disgust to his offspring:

> You would hear this from all the Argives: 'This one
> belongs to his wife (*gunaikos*), and not his wife (*gunê*) to her husband
>   (*andros*)'.
> What a disgrace to allow the woman (*gunaika*), not the man (*andra*),
> to stand as the head of the house'.[5] I hate any child
> who is known throughout the city not by virtue
> of his male father (*arsenos patros*) but of his mother (*mêtros*).
>
> > 930–35[6]

The 'pretty-boy looks' of Aegisthus represent the opposite of what Electra wants in a man, especially one who might father her sons: 'No girly-faced (*parthenôpos*) husband for me; / I want one who is manly (*andreiou*) in his looks. / For the children of such men are masters of warfare, / but the pretty sort are only fit to deck out a chorus' (948–51).[7] We sense Electra's prurient interest in the man she hates, as if she once had thought of Aegisthus as a possible husband, only to reject him because he is dominated by a woman, and looks like one.[8]

Electra berates the dead man for trusting his wife, hinting that Clytemnestra may have cheated on him (*El.* 921–24). She also accuses Aegisthus of seducing other women, but then refuses to elaborate: 'It's not a fitting subject for / a virgin' (*parthenôi*, 945 –46). In Aeschylus's *Agamemnon*, Clytemnestra levels similar charges against Agamemnon for his infidelities – 'such a soothing lover for so many Trojan girls', she says, including Cassandra, 'the woman he raped' (A. *Ag.* 1438–39). Aeschylus's Clytemnestra extends that accusation to Cassandra herself, cruelly suggesting that this captive slave girl encouraged Greek soldiers to abuse her: 'She shared his nights, / and the rowing benches with the sailors, / rubbing their "masts"' (A. *Ag.* 1441–43). A prurient interest in the sexual past of their victims seems to characterize both Aeschylus's Clytemnestra and Euripides' Electra.[9]

Like many tragic heroines, including her mother, Electra transgresses conventional gender norms. Clytemnestra reminds her daughter, 'You always loved your father – it's in your nature. / So it goes: some children are on the male side (*arsenôn*) side; / others love their mothers more than their fathers' (Eur. *El.* 1102–4).[10] Electra does more than favour the male, however; she behaves like one. Assuming the task traditionally performed by Orestes, she concocts the plan to kill Clytemnestra: 'Let me handle my mother's murder' (647).[11] At the crucial moment she takes hold of the sword along with her brother, and together they kill their mother. No other version of the murder of Clytemnestra has Electra share in the actual bloodshed.

As a married virgin, a young woman permanently stuck in the liminal state between maiden and wife, Electra represents an anomaly in the clearly structured social world of the Greeks. The ambiguity of her social and sexual identity helps explain her refusal to 'join in the chorus / of young brides of Argos' at Hera's festival (*El.* 178–79).[12] Once the princes of Greece had sought her hand in marriage; now she finds herself trapped in a sexless marriage to a farmer. With a touch of irony, the Farmer calls on Aphrodite – the goddess of erotic love – to vouch for his wife's purity and his own sexual restraint: 'She is still a virgin' (*parthenos*, 44). Orestes, however, assumes the normal state for his wedded sister: 'They say that she is yoked / in marriage, that she's no longer a virgin' (*parthenon*, 98–99). Electra sets him straight: 'My husband has never touched me in bed' (255).

In Xanthus's lost *Oresteia* (mentioned in Chapter 3), the seventh-century poet claims that the name 'Electra' (*Êlektra*) arose from a play on the word *lektron*, '(marriage) bed'. The initial *êta* ('*ê*') negates the noun that follows, a construction familiar in English in words like 'amoral', 'asexual', 'ahistorical'.[13] For the Greek audience, Electra's name carried with it the secondary meaning 'with no marriage bed', 'un-bedded', 'without sex'. Acknowledging her condition, Electra says that the citizens call her the 'wretched bed-less one [Electra]' (*athlian Êlektran*, 119).

Euripides introduces a darker aspect of male-female sexual relations with the word *hubris*. Frequently translated 'pride', *hubris* carried a more visceral punch in fifth-century Athens: 'an outrage against another', 'physical violence against someone', 'assault', 'rape'.[14] The Farmer's sense of honour and social rank prevents him from 'committing an outrage against' (i.e. 'raping', *hubrizein*, 46) his wife. Electra praises her husband for 'never taking advantage of me physically' (*enubrisas*, 68). On the other hand, she accuses Aegisthus of 'outrage' (*hubrin*) against her (58, repeated by Orestes at 266), and of 'violating' (*hubrizes*) other women (945–48). Afraid that Orestes might fail to slay Aegisthus, Electra vows to kill herself before her enemies 'utterly violate (*kathubrisai*) my body' (698).[15] Electra's fear of rape reflects real danger in a misogynist world, but it also underlines a deep sexual insecurity arising from her abnormal status as a virgin wife.

In contrast to her daughter, Clytemnestra in *Electra* is 'oversexed', and her carnal ties to Aegisthus emerge as a prominent reason for her children's hatred. Orestes wants to punish his mother 'for sharing an unholy marriage (*koinônon anosiôn gamôn*) with him' (600). Electra picks up the phrase in her invective over Aegisthus's corpse: 'You knew what kind of unholy marriage union (*anosion gêmas gamon*) you made' (926).[16] She accuses her mother of tarting herself up as soon as Agamemnon left for Troy, hoping to attract male attention. Appalled that she 'lives in sexual union with another / in her bloodstained marriage bed' (*lektrois phoniois*, 211–12), Electra cannot forgive her for having 'dishonored the bed (*lechê*) of my father' (920). The Chorus also condemn Clytemnestra's 'adulterous bed' (*sa lechea*, 481), the 'errant marriage bed' (*didromou lechous*, 1156) that cost Agamemnon his life. Speaking to Electra, the Messenger refers dismissively to Aegisthus as 'your mother's bedmate' (*mêtros eunetês*, 803). Electra picks up the term when she predicts what lies ahead for Clytemnestra: 'Soon you will be the bride in Hades' house / of the man you slept with (*xunêudes*) in the light' (1144–45).[17] She does not mean Agamemnon.

Electra compares her mother's promiscuity to that of her sister Helen, the Greek exemplar of failed female virtue. Clytemnestra herself depicts Helen as a shameless whore who ran off with Paris and betrayed her husband Menelaus, causing the death of countless Greeks and

Trojans.[18] But as Clytemnestra well knows, promiscuity goes two ways. She recalls Agamemnon's infidelities at Troy, particularly his decision to bring home his war-prize Cassandra and introduce her to their marriage bed in Argos.[19]

> ... So there were two brides
> in the same house, at the same time.
> Now women can be wayward fools, I won't deny it.
> But when a husband wanders off
> and rejects his marriage bed, his wife may want
> to follow his example and acquire a new lover.
> Yet all the blame falls on us women,
> while men, who set it off, hear nothing said against them.
>
> Eur. *El.* 1033–40

Euripides treats Clytemnestra far more sympathetically than Aeschylus or Sophocles, and her account of the double standard rings true. Passages such as this one give the lie to the claim that Euripides lacked sympathy for the situation of women in his society.[20]

Marital infidelity runs deep in the house of Atreus. In the second *stasimon*, the Chorus condemn the sexual misconduct of the previous generation, when Thyestes seduced Aerope, the wife of his brother Atreus, and seized the golden lamb. Although Euripides does not describe the aftermath, his audience knew that Atreus took revenge by tricking Thyestes into feasting on the flesh of his own children (described in Aeschylus's *Agamemnon*, 1583–1602). Recognizing the horror, Thyestes curses Atreus, and the consequences fall on Atreus's son Agamemnon. Aegisthus, the only child of Thyestes to survive, avenges his father by imitating his sexual transgression. He becomes Clytemnestra's lover, and together they assassinate Agamemnon. Aegisthus looks to secure his dynastic rule by producing a brood of children with his new wife and queen.

Aeschylus makes no mention of Aegisthus and Clytemnestra's offspring, but Sophocles' Electra assails her mother for bearing the usurper's children (S. *El.* 585–89). Euripides' Electra goes even further, for the children of her mother and Aegisthus rob her and Orestes of their rightful inheritance: 'The accursed daughter of Tyndareus, my mother, / has driven me out of my house to gratify her husband. / Begetting new children with Aegisthus, she pushes Orestes / and me aside, inherit-less subordinates in our own home' (Eur. *El.* 60–63).

On hearing that Aegisthus sacrifices to the Nymphs, Orestes asks, 'Is it for nurturing existing children, or is another child on the way?' (626). The Nymphs in question are probably the Inachides, daughters of Inachus, the river that the Farmer mentions in the first line of the play. Linked to Hera (the patron goddess of Argos), these minor deities were associated with marriage and childbirth – 'nymph' (*numphê*) also can mean 'nubile young woman', or 'bride'.[21] Euripides raises the possibility that Clytemnestra is expecting another child with Aegisthus, further threatening the patrimony that rightfully belongs to Orestes.[22]

Because tragic myths move across generations, issues of parentage and descent loom large, and *Electra* pays close attention to lineage and offspring. Consider line 60, quoted above: 'The accursed daughter of Tyndareus, my mother'. This short phrase moves from the father who engendered Clytemnestra to the mother who gave birth to Electra.[23] Although we find many references to fathers in the play, Euripides focuses on the female as the bearer of children, preparing us for the 'faux-child' scheme of Electra and the matricidal horror that is Clytemnestra's murder.

In the first *stasimon*, the Chorus sing of the shield of Achilles, identifying the Greek hero by name only once. However, they twice refer to him as 'the son of Thetis' (438, 450), honouring his goddess mother who will grieve over his death in the tenth year of the war. Clytemnestra also names Achilles, but only to emphasize the untimely death of *her* child, Iphigenia: 'My father Tyndareus did not give me to your father / so that the children I bore should be killed. / Yet he [Agamemnon] enticed my child from home / with a [fictional] marriage to Achilles, / leading her to the harbour at Aulis' (1018–22).[24] As noted in Chapter 2, Clytemnestra wonders how Agamemnon would have reacted if his brother Menelaus (rather than Helen) had been abducted to Troy, and if she had sacrificed their son Orestes to get Menelaus back.

She makes a telling point: in male-dominated Greek society, killing a daughter is one thing, a son quite another.

The maternal losses suffered by Thetis and Clytemnestra find two small but significant echoes on the pastoral level. Sent for by Electra, the Old Man brings a 'newborn lamb / pulled from the flock' (494–95) to provide a feast for the strangers.[25] In the second *stasimon*, the Chorus sing of the shepherd god Pan, who 'took a tender lamb away from its mother in the mountains / of Argos' (699–700), the 'golden lamb' that represents political power in Argos. These passages do not imply that the Greeks held sentimental views about livestock, but they do specify the separation of the young from their mothers. In Aeschylus's *Agamemnon*, Clytemnestra uses the same image to describe how Agamemnon killed her daughter Iphigenia, as if 'slaughtering a lamb / when his flocks teemed with sheep' (A. *Ag.* 1415–16).[26]

Given the importance of the matricide in *Electra*, it is hardly surprising that Euripides emphasizes children and childbearing. In relation to Clytemnestra's maternity, he frequently uses a form of the verb *tekein* ('to give birth') in addition to, or in place of, the more generic *mêtêr* ('mother').[27] Electra says 'I am born (*egenoman*) of Agamemnon, / and Clytemnestra gave me birth' (*m' etikte*, Eur. *El.* 115–16). Orestes asks Electra, 'Did the mother who bore you (*mêtêr de s' hê tekousa*) allow your marriage to happen?' (264). In the decisive dialogue between Orestes and Electra (961–77), *mêtêr* ('mother') or a comparable term occurs eight times in seventeen lines.[28] Electra announces the arrival of 'the woman who bore me and gave me birth' (*tên tekousan hê m' egeinato*, 965). A hesitant Orestes wonders how he can kill 'the woman who bore me and raised me'? (*hê m' ethrepse k'ateken*, 969). After the murder, Electra repents of having raged with such hatred against 'my mother, / who gave me birth as her daughter' (*matri taid', / ha m' etikte kouran*, 1183–84). The Chorus identify the fatal web that ties Clytemnestra to her progeny: 'Unforgettable the children you bore as a mother (*mater tekous'*) / and more than unforgettable / what you suffered from your offspring' (*sôn teknôn*, 1186–88). Standing over his mother's corpse, Orestes captures the simple, tragic irony: 'You gave birth to your own killers' (*phoneas etiktes*, 1229).

By inventing a newborn child to lure Clytemnestra to her death, Electra puts the unnaturalness of matricide in high relief. 'Tell her I bore a male' (*arsenos tokôi*, 652), she says, thinking that Clytemnestra will come 'to weep at the low status of my child' (*emôn tokôn*, 658).[29] Her mother makes the journey, but she fails to behave as Electra predicts. Clytemnestra says nothing about her grandson's father or the newborn's social inferiority. Rather, she notes with dismay her daughter's isolation and poverty: 'And you, unwashed, your body in rags / after just giving birth?' (*neognôn ek tokôn*, 1107–8).[30] She wonders where the women are who 'delivered the baby' (*ek tokôn*, 1128). Electra answers that she had no midwife and 'bore (*ka'tekon*) this infant alone' (1129).

Why does Clytemnestra come to Electra's cottage? Guilt for her past actions, the need to state her case to her daughter, pity for Electra's condition, concern for ritual propriety, and grand-maternal instincts all seem to play a part.[31] Clytemnestra says that she offers her help as a 'gift' or 'grace' (*charin*, 1133) for her daughter, before she 'graces' (*charin*, 1138) her husband's sacrifice to the Nymphs (Chapter 5). Earlier Electra claimed that 'women love their husbands, not their children' (265), but in this scene, Clytemnestra tries to do both.

Two details in Clytemnestra's offstage murder bring home the disturbing connection between the (false) childbirth and the matricide. Before she dies, Clytemnestra bares her breast, forcing Orestes to confront the fact that he is about to kill the woman who bore and nursed him. Her gesture points to the famous scene in Aeschylus's *Choephori* when Clytemnestra does the same thing, crying out 'My son, my child, / pity the breast where you dozed, your gums / sucking the milk that nourished you' (A. *Cho.* 896–98).[32] Euripides adds an even more intimate appeal. Orestes describes how his mother sprawled on the ground, exposing 'the limbs that gave me birth' (1209).[33] The ensuing spilled blood brings to mind the bleeding that accompanies childbirth,[34] suggesting that Electra's virtual 'delivery' has merged with her own mother's lifeblood.

Having presented his protagonist as both a married virgin and a childless mother, Euripides tries to set things straight at the end. Once

Electra's suitor and now a demigod, Castor tells Orestes to release his sister from her marriage to the Farmer: 'Let Pylades ... take Electra with him / as virgin and wife' (1284–85). Orestes highlights her soon-to-be-lost chastity, telling Pylades: 'Go with blessings, and wed / the body of Electra' (*numpheuou / demas Êlektras*, 1340–41).[35] However, the prospect of union with Pylades fails to lift the spirits of the bride-to-be. Electra expresses grief at the separation from her brother, and from Argos; she says nothing about the married life that lies ahead, or the fulfilment that she once had longed for as a much-wooed princess.[36]

As we shall see in Chapter 9, some adaptations of the Electra story develop her more-than-sisterly attachment to Orestes. Euripides scatters a few details that support this possibility, particularly Electra's inflated opinion of her brother's physical qualities, his masculine persona, and his heroic character. Orestes also implies that stronger-than- normal bonds draw them together: 'You were young when you were separated [literally 'unyoked', *apezeuchthês*] from Orestes' (284). Electra returns to this figure of speech at the end of the play: 'The curse of mother's murder unyokes us (*dia ... zeugnus'*) / from our father's house' (1323–24). Tragedians frequently employ the metaphor of yoking for a wedding or a wedded pair, and Euripides implies that association here.[37]

In *Electra*, Euripides brings together an array of gender-bending contradictions and sexually charged paradoxes. A chaste husband, a married virgin; an adulterous wife, and her seductive but effeminate lover, then husband; childlessness, murdered offspring, and an imaginary son and grandson; sexual rivalries, marital infidelities, and invectives against promiscuity and double standards; excessive glorification of masculinity and fear of male physical assault; women who behave like men and vice-versa; a festival for maidens and for newlyweds, rejected by a heroine who is neither and both; belated maternal affection and deadly filial hatred; fabricated childbirth and the real blood of a murdered mother. Given the explosion of current interest (from genetic research to identity politics) in questions surrounding gender and sexuality, Euripides' *Electra* seems very much our contemporary.[38]

Highs and Lows in *Electra*

Rich and Poor, Gods and Mortals, Sky and Earth

During tragic performances at the City Dionysia, audiences witnessed mythic characters in situations far exceeding the norms of daily life: revenge, assassination, human sacrifice, matricide, epic warfare, conflicts between gods and mortals (usually with lethal consequences). At the same time, the performances drew on legal, religious, social, and cultural practices that reflected contemporary Athenian society. As in other tragedies of Euripides, *Electra* uses the differences between the mythic realm and the world of fifth-century Athens to explore – and expose – values inherent in each.

When the Farmer entered and launched the prologue, the original audience in the theatre of Dionysus must have wondered, 'What is Euripides *doing*? Why has he set the story we all know in front of this poor Farmer's cottage?'[1] The sense of not belonging, of displacement, extends to the principal characters. Electra sees her life on the farm as a violation of her rightful position in the palace, and her role as a peasant's wife an insult to her aristocratic birth. At first sight, Orestes takes his sister for some slave woman tasked with bringing water from the spring. When he learns the truth, and Electra's husband welcomes him into their humble abode, he wishes that he – and the real Orestes – were entering the palace and not a peasant's hovel.[2]

The opposition between wealth and poverty, nobility and low birth, and luxury and labour runs through the play. Electra tells her regally dressed mother that 'paupers (*penêtas*) have no friends' (*El.* 1131), and she warns Clytemnestra to be careful when entering 'our impoverished (*penêtas*) house' (1139).[3] Earlier Electra describes her husband as

Fig. 6 Elektra (Irene Pappas) and Peasant (Notis Periyalis), from *Elektra* (1962), directed by Michael Cacoyannis. Courtesy of the Michael Cacoyannis Foundation.

'a poor man (*penês*) but noble (*gennaios*)' (253), and the Farmer says the same of himself: 'Although I am poor (*penês*), / I will show you no ignobility (*dusgenes*) of character' (362–63). He knows that 'a full stomach / is the same, whether one is rich (*plousios*) or poor (*penês*)' (430–31). Orestes doubts that either prosperity or poverty guarantees excellence of character: 'Wealth (*ploutôi*) is poor criteria' (374), for it can disguise the faults of pride and cowardice. On the other hand, 'poverty (*penia*) is a disease, / that teaches men to be evil out of necessity'

(375–76). In the end, Orestes says that he prefers 'a poor (*penês*) host / who is eager, to a wealthy one (*plousiou*) who is not' (394–95).

The social and economic tensions in Euripides' Athens lie behind these passages: the challenge to hereditary prerogatives posed by Athenian democracy; the rise of self-made citizens (merchants, politicians, artisans) at the expense of the old aristocracy; doubts about the causal link between high birth and good character, and the possibility that nobility lies in behaviour rather than privilege.[4] More than any other extant Greek tragedy, *Electra* challenges the assumptions that wealth is self-validating, and that poverty in itself signals idleness and moral weakness.[5] Although the social upheavals of fifth-century Athens may seem remote to us, we are experiencing a similar disjunction caused by our political-economic system that enables great prosperity for the few at the expense of the many, particularly those 'at the bottom'.

Reflecting the interests of different economic and social strata, Euripides' characters frequently employ mercantile language and financial metaphors, which seem at odds with the play's mythic context. Before pursuing his revenge, Orestes assumes he must act alone because he is 'bankrupt of friends' (*El.* 601–2). The Messenger views the murder of Aegisthus as 'blood for blood, / the bitter paying back of a loan' (857–58), long overdue for the children of Agamemnon. As noted in Chapter 5, the colour gold occurs frequently (golden sun, golden temples, golden lamb, the golden face of dawn), but it also refers to mere lucre: Aegisthus offers gold as financial reward for anyone who kills Orestes. Electra rejects the view that riches in themselves have long-term value, or that they can purchase anything that does. She assails Aegisthus for boasting that his 'money' (*chrêmasi*, 939) compensates for his lack of character. He should have known that 'wealth doesn't last, / but only blossoms for a short spell, and then flies away' (943–44). Although Clytemnestra sees her Trojan slaves as 'beautiful possessions for the house' (1003), Electra accuses her of 'buying her husband' Aegisthus for the price of their ancestral home (1089–90).

This 'money talk' finds its down-to-earth counterpart in the words of the Farmer. 'With respect to money / I am poor' (*chrêmatôn* ... /

penêtes, 37–38), he admits, but he displays qualities of forbearance, respect, and open-heartedness. The only innocent character in the play, he knows nothing of palace life, has played no part in its bloody past, and has no knowledge of the actual plan to kill Aegisthus and Clytemnestra. When Electra sends him off to fetch the Tutor, he leaves the stage, never to return.[6] His absence allows the former inhabitants of the house of Atreus – Electra, Orestes, and the Tutor – to turn his poor cottage into the home of a non-existent infant, a temporary storeroom for Aegisthus's corpse, and the setting for Clytemnestra's ambush by her own children.

As we would expect in Greek tragedy, the earthly concerns of humans – from poverty to payback – inevitably involve the 'higher-ups' on Olympus. Gods and demigods are all over *Electra* – the word *theos* ('god', the root of our 'theology') occurs more than twenty times in the play.[7] A host of divinities are mentioned by name, most of them more than once: Aphrodite, Ares, Pan, Moira (Fate), and Night, once each; Athena, Hera, Gaia (Earth), Keres (Furies), and the Nereids (sea nymphs), twice; Hades and Dike (Justice), three times; the Nymphs (female deities associated with water, marriage, and fertility), five times; Zeus, nine times; and Apollo, fifteen times. As happens in most plays of Euripides, *Electra* ends with the actual appearance of a god on high. The deified sons of Zeus, Castor and Polydeuces, comment on what has transpired and attempt to provide closure to the tragic events of the play. Some scholars think they succeed; others find the efforts of the immortal twins so inadequate that they undermine the wisdom, and even the credibility, of the divine forces behind the myth.[8]

In Euripides' *Heracles*, the title character condemns the goddess Hera, who struck him with madness that made him slay his wife and children: 'Who would offer prayers / to such a goddess? ... / ... She destroyed a man who accomplished / great things for Greece, a man who was guiltless' (*HF* 1307–10). We find similar statements about the gods in *Electra*, revealing a fundamental gap between the immortals' perspective on events and the experience of the humans caught up in them.[9] For some scholars, such passages demonstrate the limited range of human vision, and they conclude that Euripides never seriously questions belief in the gods or challenges their role as ultimate arbiters of human affairs. From this perspective, issues of divine right and wrong are irrelevant – the Olympians exercise a level of power and authority that humans cannot understand, but would be fools to question.[10]

When Electra rejects the Chorus's invitation to join them at the festival of Hera, the maidens respond that the goddess is great, and that by honouring her Electra will get the help she needs more effectively than by lamenting her misfortunes. Electra insists that no gods hear her prayers, for they have not responded to her father's murder and her brother's exile. We may compare her despair regarding the justice of the gods with her brother's initial faith in the word of Apollo: 'The oracles of Apollo are steadfast, / but I reject prophecies from mere mortals' (*El.* 399–400). Orestes bases his belief in the gods on their commitment to his and Electra's cause: 'No longer should we believe in the gods / if injustice [the murder of Agamemnon] triumphs over justice [revenge on Aegisthus and Clytemnestra]' (583–84). Before embarking on the first stage of their revenge, he and Electra pray to Zeus and Hera for success: 'Grant us victory, if our prayer is just' (675). Confirming Orestes' triumph, the Messenger announces to Electra and the Chorus, 'Now we must offer prayers of thanksgiving to the gods' (764).

Once the matricide approaches, however, Orestes questions his earlier conviction: 'Apollo, there was no wisdom when you prophesied. / ... You commanded me to kill someone I must not, my mother. / ... / Did some destructive spirit speak disguised as a god? / ... / I cannot believe that such a prophecy was good' (971–73, 979–81). Electra dismisses her brother's startling reversal as nothing more than cowardice. After the event, however, she too questions the gods: 'What kind of Apollo, what sort of oracle / made me into the murderer of my mother?' (1303–4).[11] Castor tries to convince Orestes and Electra that the murder of Clytemnestra was not their fault: 'I ascribe this act of bloodshed / to Apollo' (1296–97). In almost the same breath, he criticizes the god and his oracle: 'Fate and Necessity and the unwise words / of Apollo directed the destined outcome' (1301–2).

For all the talk of Apollo, his oracle plays a far less significant role in Euripides' tragedy than in Aeschylus's *Choephori* or Sophocles' *Electra*. Aeschylus's Orestes describes a list of horrors that Apollo will inflict on him if he fails to kill his mother (A. *Cho.* 269–97). The opening of *Eumenides*, the third play of Aeschylus's trilogy, takes place at the god's temple in Delphi, where Orestes takes refuge from the Furies. Apollo appears in person to protect him, and he reappears to defend Orestes at his trial in Athens. Sophocles' *Electra* opens with Orestes having just consulted the Delphic oracle. Orestes' 'false death', narrated by the Tutor, involves a fatal accident in a chariot race at the Pythian games in Delphi, held in Apollo's honour. Sophocles burnishes the god's role by having Electra pray to Apollo to aid in the matricide just before it takes place.

In his *Electra*, however, Euripides minimizes Apollo's presence and importance. When Castor tries to blame the god rather than Electra and Orestes for the matricide, one hears special pleading. Even the killers refuse to embrace Castor's dismissal of their responsibility, and they remain unpersuaded that what lies ahead for them – a new husband for Electra and a new city for Orestes – is what they want, or should want.

The audience, too, may have a hard time swallowing the happy ending announced by Castor. Recall that the Dioskouroi also reveal the truth about the Trojan War. Zeus, greatest of the gods, instigated the conflict 'to cause unrest and bloodshed among mortals' (1282). Whatever heroics arose from that ten-year conflict now seem absurd: 'Deeds of bravery and courage for *what*? To recover Helen, who never set foot in Troy?' Whether taking the blame for something they didn't do (Apollo), or tricking mortals into a meaningless war (Zeus), the gods pose an intractable problem for the human characters in *Electra*.

So who were the gods and what did they represent? In the polytheism of ancient Greece, the gods had multiple cults, many of which linked their power and influence to natural phenomena. Zeus had almost a hundred different cult titles, connected to a broad range of elements, activities, and places – rain, darkness, lightning, thunder, moisture, dust, fair winds, harvest, friendship, guests and hospitality, suppliants, deliverance, victory in battle, the market place, the household hearth, the city council, oak forests, tall mountains.[12] Ancient Greek religion was grounded in the physical environment, lending a play like *Electra* an ecological dimension, bound up in the (often fraught) relationship between humans and their divinely infused surroundings.

In Chapters 3 and 4, we touched on the workmanlike concerns of the Farmer, aware of the watershed and the changing seasons, ready to begin his spring ploughing and sowing at dawn, working with his animals to eke out a living. His cottage is surrounded (at least verbally) by nature: the rocky hillside, the Inachus river below, the fields, the freshwater spring, and so on. So, too, the hills where the Old Man tends his flocks and the meadows where Aegisthus rears his horses – both belong more to the natural world than to the Argive palace, the traditional backdrop for the story.[13] Visible and audible parallels to the verbal descriptions in the play appeared to Euripides' audience in the theatre of Dionysus, introduced in Chapter 1: Mt. Hymettus dominating the horizon to the east; the Ilissos river glistening much closer, to the south-east; the Saronic Gulf opening up to the Peloponnese to the south and west; the braying donkeys in the farms just outside the city walls below the theatre; the horses whinnying behind the stage façade, yoked to the wagon and waiting for their entrance with Clytemnestra and her Trojan slaves.

The characters and Chorus in *Electra* also look up towards the heavens. On her first entrance, before addressing anything or anyone else, Electra calls on the night and the golden stars (54). Because Agamemnon's tomb lies far from the cottage, the site cannot serve as the locus for Electra's grief, so she laments to the sky above. At the end of his opening speech, Orestes announces the rising sun (102), and the Chorus interpret his homecoming as the 'long-awaited day / dawning' over Argos (585–86), freeing them from the benighted rule of the tyrant Aegisthus. Fabricating her murder plot, Electra claims that she gave birth to her baby 'ten suns ago' (654), a story she repeats to Clytemnestra, replacing 'suns' with 'moons' (1126).[14] Electra's use of celestial bodies to mark temporal change reminds us that the ancients maintained a primary connection between natural phenomena and the passage of time, something we tend to forget when we speak of days and months and years that lie ahead of, or behind us.[15]

To grasp the degree to which the heavens matter in *Electra*, let us return to the two great lyric *stasima* of the Chorus. In the first, the women describe engravings on Achilles' shield, in the centre of which shine bright celestial bodies: the chariot of the sun surrounded by a chorus of stars, the Pleiades and Hyades (464–69), which formed the eyes and shoulder of the constellation Taurus (the Bull).[16] Associated with the spring rains, the mythical Hyades were a sisterhood of nymphs, all of them daughters of Atlas, one of the Titans who revolted against Zeus and the Olympian gods. Atlas also fathered a second group of daughters, the Pleiades (probably derived from the Greek verb 'to sail', *plein*), also known as the 'Seven Sisters'. These stars appeared in the Mediterranean sky in the spring, rising above the eastern horizon to announce the opening of the sailing season.[17]

Brightest among these Seven Sisters was Maia, the mother of the god Hermes. The Chorus refer to both her and her son when they describe the images on the outer rim of Achilles' shield: 'Perseus skims over the sea on winged sandals / holding the severed head of the Gorgon / along with Hermes, the messenger of Zeus, / the country-wild son of Maia' (459–62). The Messenger invokes the same myth when he compares Orestes' murder of Aegisthus to Perseus's slaying the Gorgon (discussed in Chapter 6), leading some to conclude that the 'arms of Achilles' ode offers a heroic analogy to Orestes' eventual encounter with Aegisthus and Clytemnestra.[18]

This interpretation seems correct as far as it goes, but the images spiralling around Achilles' shield set off a wider range of associations. The rainmaking Hyades (depicted in the shield's centre) help feed the spring where Electra fetches water, and they nourish the horse pasture and 'well-watered garden' (777) where Orestes kills Aegisthus. Their welcome rain would swell the Inachus river (1) that irrigates the farmer's fields; the Tanaus River (410) where the Old Man tends his flock; the

Simois that flows through Troy (441); the Alpheus that borders Olympia (781, 793–94, 863) and that runs through the city that Orestes will found (1273–75).[19] As for the Pleiades, their appearance in spring roughly coincided with the City Dionysia, held when the Aegean Sea grew more hospitable to those travelling from afar.[20] Described as 'saviours / to men in the midst of the salt waves' (992–93), Castor and Polydeuces depart at the end of the play for the seas around Sicily. There, they will continue their mission of protecting sailors (1347–55) who depended – as all Greeks knew – on the stars to mark the seasons and steer their ships.

Given the primitive technology of the ancient Greeks, and their relative powerlessness before the forces of nature, it is not surprising that they held a more numinous view of the environment than we do.[21] One sees this clearly in the Chorus' second *stasimon*, which posits a causal link among human actions, divine intervention, and the motion of celestial bodies. The Chorus recount 'an age-old legend' (701) about a golden lamb, torn from its mother and brought to Argos as a sign of the city's rightful ruler. To punish Thyestes for stealing the lamb, Zeus reverses the course of the sun, altering its direction across the sky and causing a radical change in the earth's climate.[22]

> Then, then it was that Zeus
> changed the path of the glowing stars,
> reversed the course of the shining sun,
> pale glowing face of dawn.
> Now the sun drives westward, laying
> a god-kindled flame along the back
> of the sky, while the rain-filled clouds
> head north. Now the African plains
> lie fallow, parched, dying of thirst,
> robbed of the lush spring rains of Zeus.
>
> Well, that's how the story
> goes, but I don't put much faith in
> old wives' tales … really! … That the sun
> would change, speed its molten face of gold
> the other way, because of mortals'

folly, or for their punishment!
But such myths do profit men by
teaching them to fear and serve the gods,
the gods you forgot, Clytemnestra, when you killed
your husband, you, sister of such glorious brothers.[23]

El. 727–46

Performed between Orestes' departure and the Messenger's arrival, the second *stasimon* covers the offstage murder of Aegisthus, tying his misdeeds to those of his father Thyestes. Both unseated the rightful Argive king (Agamemnon/Atreus) by seducing his queen (Clytemnestra/Aerope), and both stand justly condemned.

However, the Chorus direct the last lines of their lyric at Clytemnestra ('you didn't listen'), and they do the same at the close of the first *stasimon*: 'Your adulterous bed / killed the leader of such great / warriors ... / May I see your neck gone, as once more / the iron blade gushes deep crimson' (479–81, 485–86). Both lyric narratives propel the action specifically towards matricide. As that prospect approaches, however, Orestes wonders whether the gods have acted wisely in urging this revenge, and he, Electra, and the Chorus express their horror once the murder of Clytemnestra takes place.

Let us approach their shift in attitude towards the matricide by considering the Chorus's earlier doubts about the story of the sun's reversal. At the turning point in the lyric (737–46), the young women abandon their role as engaged narrators of received legend and become sceptics who question its veracity.[24] In so doing, they anticipate the distancing that Electra and Orestes feel after committing themselves to their traditional roles as avengers of their father's murder. Their change of heart, from driven executioners to appalled murderers, represents a profound re-thinking of the entire Orestes/Electra myth. Along with them, we (as readers and audience) may question the necessity and morality of the story these characters have found themselves in.

In his volume on Euripides' *Orestes* in this series, Matthew Wright coins the term 'meta-mythological' for this troubling aspect of Euripides' tragedies, which aims 'to problematize the concept of myth

itself'.[25] In *Electra*, the *coup de grâce* of this attack on myth comes with
Castor's revelation about the Trojan War: 'Helen will help with the
burial, having left Egypt / and the house of Proteus [the Egyptian king].
She never went to Troy. / In order to bring strife and death to mortals,
Zeus / fashioned an image of Helen and sent it to Troy' (*El.* 1280–83).
In four lines, Euripides exposes the mythic justification for the great
Trojan War as nothing but a god-sent delusion.

We should not underestimate the fallout from this revelation, which
casts a long shadow over the play we have seen.[26] Orestes and Electra
learn that their father unwittingly led his men to war for no other
reason than to satisfy Zeus's desire for 'strife and death'. What are we to
make of the 'arms of Achilles' chorus that celebrated the Greek fleet's
departure for Troy, or of Electra's invective against Aegisthus for *not*
fighting in the war? Or of Orestes' summoning his father for help, to
'come with all your dead allies, / all those who helped you wipe out Troy
by the spear' (680–81)? Agamemnon's sacrifice of Iphigenia appears
even more unwarranted than Clytemnestra imagined in her speech to
Electra. In so far as the murder of Iphigenia drove her to kill her
husband, Clytemnestra's revenge and her subsequent death at the hands
of her children appear as collateral damage in a gratuitous war that
accomplished nothing but the loss of human life. Clytemnestra kills
Agamemnon for sacrificing their child so that he could wage war for a
phantom; Electra kills her mother by luring her to offer sacrifice for a
grandchild who doesn't exist.

Orestes and Electra make no response to Castor's news that Zeus
started the Trojan War to cause havoc for the human race. But they
continue to express their anguish over killing their mother, asking why
Apollo and the gods allowed it to happen. Castor insists that they look
on the bright side, reminding Electra that she has 'a husband and a
home' (1311) and urging Orestes to 'cheer up, for you are going to the
holy city / of Athena' (1319–20). Castor's efforts to throw a positive light
on what has transpired fail to brighten the mood.[27] His physical
separation from those below reflects an unbridgeable gap between
divine perspectives and human experience.

Euripides forces us to question the cosmic reaction to the golden lamb, the need to murder Clytemnestra, and the justification for the Trojan War. Nevertheless, these myths continue to make meaningful contact with audiences, ancient and modern. In the twenty-first century, we might find ourselves agreeing with the Chorus in the second *stasimon*, concluding (as they do) that if we imagined our actions had large-scale consequences, we would think twice before we performed them.

The story of the sun shifting course and drastically changing the earth's ecology might prompt us to reconsider the contemporary myth that 'progress' depends on environmental degradation. Although powerful forces are aligned against any change, we know that if we continue to burn fossil fuels, destroy biodiversity, level forests, poison the air, and pollute the seas and the land, then we threaten the survival of human life on earth. At the end of Euripides' play, Electra and Orestes wish they had resisted the myth that they were swept up in. Their belated awareness might speak to us, as we realize what lies in store if we don't break out of our inherited narrative.

In Aristophanes' *Frogs*, Euripides describes his tragedies as teaching people 'to suspect everything'.[28] *Electra* may not go that far, but Burian points out that the play forces 'the audience to rethink every facet of character, motivation, and the very meaning of the action'.[29] *Electra* exposes the fault lines between heroic ideals and everyday life, between those who have inherited privilege and status and those who work in the fields, between the perspective of powerful gods and the aspirations of vulnerable mortals, between the artifice of the theatre and the messier world that the stage represents.

The nineteenth-century English poet Algernon Swinburne wrote that great tragedy (Aeschylus, Shakespeare) deals with 'the grave and deep truth of natural impulse', but in Euripides this theme is often 'outraged and degraded by the vulgar theatricalities'.[30] Perhaps Swinburne was thinking of Electra's self-dramatization, the grotesque murder of Aegisthus, or the sordid nature of the matricide. As we shall see in the closing chapter, later versions of the play often emphasize these elements, as if they represent the best *Electra* has to offer. One can imagine a Hollywood agent pitching Euripides' play as an innovative hybrid – eroticized melodrama and slasher film – but one that merits a GP ('General Public') rating due to its classical pedigree.

In my view, Euripides' 'vulgar theatricalities' add immeasurably to the moral and emotional effect on his audience, part and parcel of what makes *Electra* such a powerful and disturbing tragedy. Like Orestes and Electra at the end of the play, we may find ourselves caught between the bloodshed on the ground and the distant movement of the heavens, looking for hopeful signs of divine intervention as we grapple with the losses we have brought on ourselves, and the exile that lies ahead for many of us on the planet.

Electra through the Looking Glass

... and the repeated air
Of sad Electra's Poet had the pow'r
To save th'Athenian Walls from ruine bare.

John Milton[1]

The lines of John Milton's sonnet refer to an anecdote from the Greek biographer and essayist Plutarch (46–*c.* 120 AD). At the end of the Peloponnesian War (404 BC), he tells us, the victorious Spartan generals planned to raze the city of Athens, but they changed their minds when someone sang the opening of the *parodos* of Euripides' *Electra*. The conquerors then decided it would be wrong to destroy a city that had produced so great a poet.[2]

This chapter explores the afterlife of Euripides' play – translations, productions, and adaptations inspired or shaped by the original. The many performances of his tragedies at the City Dionysia attest to Euripides' popularity in the last half of the fifth century BC, as do the frequent references to the playwright in the comedies of Aristophanes.[3] From the fourth century BC through the heyday of the Roman Empire, Euripides proved the most popular source for theatrical revivals and adaptations, more so than Aeschylus and Sophocles; however, his *Electra* was not among the favoured plays.[4] Sometime between the fourth and ninth centuries AD, scholars and educators compiled the so-called 'select' plays of Euripides, chosen on the basis of performance popularity (often as excerpts rather than full plays), the needs of school curricula, their usefulness for rhetorical training, and the perceived relevance of their mythological content.[5] Again, *Electra* was not in this group. Our play survived due to the accidental transmission of Euripides' 'alphabetic' plays, which included titles beginning with the

Greek letter *epsilon* through *kappa*, into which *Electra* falls. For over
two millennia after its fifth-century BC premiere at the City Dionysia,
no significant translation, production, or adaptation of Euripides'
Electra left its mark.

A remarkable change in the fortunes of the play occurred in 1905
with the English translation by Sydney-born, Oxford-educated Gilbert
Murray (1866–1957). Professor of Greek at the University of Glasgow
and later Regius Professor of Greek at Oxford, Murray was something
of a Renaissance man who maintained a strong interest in contemporary
theatre.[6] The success of his translations of Euripides arose in no small
part from their association with a theatrical movement that had taken
off a few decades earlier. Playwrights involved with this 'new theatre'
include Henrik Ibsen, August Strindberg, Anton Chekhov, Gerhart
Hauptmann, Arthur Schnitzler, Franz Wedekind, John Millington
Synge, George Bernard Shaw, and (somewhat later) Eugene O'Neill.
Smaller theatres dedicated to the new drama mushroomed in European
capitals – Théâtre Libre in Paris, the Freie Bühne in Berlin, the Art
Theatre in Moscow, the Abbey Theatre in Dublin, the Court (later the
Royal Court) in London. This last theatre played a major role in
restoring Euripides' *Electra* to the stage.

Murray translated several of Euripides' tragedies, which his friend
Bernard Shaw urged him to publish after hearing Murray read from
them at a Fabian Society meeting in London in 1901.[7] Shaw ushered
Murray into the London theatrical scene, and he befriended the young
Harley Granville Barker, who directed Murray's translation of Euripides'
Hippolytus in London in 1904.[8] Later that same year, Barker became
manager of the Court Theatre in Sloane Square, inaugurating his tenure
with a new production of *Hippolytus* (again Murray's translation). Over
the next three seasons (1904–7), Granville Barker produced (and often
directed and acted in) an impressive number of productions, including
eleven plays by Shaw and three by Euripides – *Hippolytus, Trojan
Women,* and *Electra,* all in Murray's translations – making Euripides
the second most produced playwright during Barker's transformative
years at the Court.[9]

Among the many Shaw productions, Barker directed *Major Barbara* (1905), in which he also played the role of Adolphus Cusins, a high-minded classicist based on Gilbert Murray. At the end of *Major Barbara*, Cusins overcomes his scruples about the armaments business:

> You cannot have power for good without having power for evil too. Even mother's milk nourishes murderers as well as heroes ... I want a power simple enough for common men to use, yet strong enough to force the intellectual oligarchy to use its genius for the general good ... Dare I make war on war? I dare. I must. I will.[10]

One detects a Euripidean undercurrent here, and many at the time perceived a strong connection between Shaw and Euripides, viewed as the ironists and iconoclasts of their respective epochs.[11]

Barker, Murray, Shaw, and the Court Theatre offered a springboard for approaching Euripides as a modern playwright rather than an ancient Greek author, one who spoke to contemporary audiences. *Electra* entered the twentieth-century English theatre less as a timeworn classic than as a play for the modern moment. Such was the view of theatre critic Desmond MacCarthy in 1907:

> Mr. Gilbert Murray's rare and beautiful translations of Euripides proved that ... the old Greek dramas could be refashioned into plays that the English reader might enjoy and understand with the same close, effortless sympathy with which he might follow the work of a modern imagination ... Mr. Murray had turned Euripides into an English poet-dramatist ... Barker tried what could be done towards naturalizing him on the English stage.[12]

One should be wary of echoing MacCarthy's enthusiasm for Murray's translations uncritically.[13] Consider, for example, his rendering of the opening lines of *Electra*, spoken by the Farmer:

> Old gleam on the face of the world, I give thee hail,
> River of Argos land, where sail on sail
> The long ships met, a thousand, near and far,
> When Agamemnon walked the seas in war;
> Who smote King Priam in the dust, and burned

The storied streets of Ilion, and returned
Above all conquerors, heaping tower and fane
Of Argos high with spoils of Eastern slain.[14]

Rhyming couplets (Greek tragedians did not use rhyme), flowery elaboration, and inappropriate Victorian diction hardly serve the play. Nonetheless, Murray's translations helped establish Euripides as the most contemporary of ancient tragedians.[15]

Following the success of Euripides at the Court, Euripides' *Electra* received numerous professional productions across the globe.[16] The first modern-Greek production of the play, staged in 1924 at the indoor Royal (later National) Theatre in Athens, featured Angeliki Kotsali as Electra, a role she reprised in 1927 and 1930 at the outdoor Odeon of Herodes Atticus. A stone's throw from the original theatre of Dionysus, where Euripides staged his *Electra*, this Roman theatre (seating roughly 5,000) became one of the main performance spaces for the Athens and Epidaurus Festivals, launched in 1955. The major venue of the Festival remains the late fourth-century BC theatre at Epidaurus (seating roughly 13,000).

The most acclaimed modern-Greek production of Euripides' *Electra* took place at Epidaurus in 1989, directed by Kostas Tsianos, with Lydia Koniordou in the title role.[17] Tsianos began as a dancer with the Dora Stratou Company, renowned for performing traditional music and folk dance from across the Greek world. He moved into the theatre as an actor and director; his mentor Dimitris Rontiris had mounted the first modern staging of a Greek tragedy at Epidaurus in 1938.[18]

Fitting for a play set in the country, far from the centre of political power, Tsianos's production of *Electra* began in a regional theatre of Larissa before moving to Epidaurus. Its extraordinary success helped validate regional theatre in what had been an Athenocentric cultural landscape. Incorporating music, costume, and dance from the Greek folk tradition, Tsianos opened up new possibilities for the tragic Chorus. In the title role, Lydia Koniordou harnessed the raw dramatic power of Euripides' troubled protagonist (see Figure 2).[19] A triumph in Greece, the production toured internationally from 1991 to 1993, allowing non-Greek audiences to experience ancient tragedy that drew on popular performance traditions rather than dated assumptions about 'classical style'.

In spite of Tsianos's influence, many contemporary productions of Euripides' *Electra* tend to sacrifice rootedness in community in favour of cinematic effects, using graphic visuals to bring home the offstage violence of the original. In his 2019 Comédie-Française production *Électre/Oreste*, for example, director Ivo van Hove placed the Farmer's cottage in a field of mud, with a slightly elevated walkway allowing for entrances from the distance. As the play moved to matricide, the mud gradually covered the bodies of Electra and Orestes, mixed with Clytemnestra's blood. 'Forget *Game of Thrones*! Nobody does violence like Euripides!' proclaimed the headline of the *New York Times* review: 'With her cropped hair and tattered shorts, Ms. Brahim cuts an androgynous figure, who doesn't just maim Clytemnestra's lover, Aegisthus, but bites into his dismembered genitals before throwing

Fig. 7 Chorus member, Oreste (Christophe Montenez), and Électre (Suliane Brahim), with corpse of Clytemnestre (Elsa Lepoivre), Chorus in background, from the 2019 Comédie-Française production *Électre/Oreste*, directed by Ivan van Hove. Courtesy of Comédie Française.

them at the Chorus.[20] Van Hove took the verbal energy of Euripides and replaced it with physical and visual excess. Supported by an onstage percussion quartet, the choreography by Wim Vandekeybus added to the sense of wildness in the Chorus and Electra, well suited to the play's subject, if not exactly to Euripides' treatment of it.

Turning from theatrical productions of Euripides' *Electra* to significant adaptations of the play, the American poet Robinson Jeffers published a long dramatic poem dealing with the house of Atreus, *The Tower beyond Tragedy*, in 1925.[21] Educated in Greek and Latin from an early age, Jeffers (1887–1962) based the first half of his drama on Aeschylus's *Agamemnon*, then increasingly drew on Euripides as the plot turned to matricide.

Years after Agamemnon's murder, a beggar shows up at the palace, her face covered in filth – Electra in disguise. Aegisthus tells Clytemnestra to treat kindly 'this poor creature on the step who has been reared nicely and slipped into misery'.[22] After revealing her identity, Electra gives her mother the false news that Orestes has died, a plot device borrowed from Aeschylus and Sophocles. In the scene between mother and daughter, however, we see Euripides' influence writ large. A repentant Clytemnestra asks for understanding and reconciliation: 'Electra, / Make peace with me. . . . / I have labored violently all the days of my life for nothing – / nothing worse than anything – this death / Was a thing I wished. See how they [the Gods] make fools of us. / Amusement for them, to watch us labor after the thing that will / tear us in / pieces . . .'[23]

Once Orestes arrives, Electra spurs her brother to matricide, just as she does in Euripides' play. Orestes hesitates, asking again and again if he should 'Dip in my sword / Into my fountain?' (*Tower* 69). His sister berates him and calls him a coward, until he reluctantly slays Clytemnestra. A triumphant Electra announces the return of Agamemnon's son as rightful king, but Orestes has no interest in power and wishes to leave the city. Developing the sexual theme hinted at in Euripides, Electra offers herself to her brother, trying to persuade him not to go: 'O will you stay! these arms / Making so soft and white a bond around you . . . I also begin to love you that way, Orestes, / Feeling the hot hard flesh move under the loose cloth, shudder against me ... Ah, your mouth, Ah, / The burning – kiss me'.[24]

Orestes rejects her advances, saying: 'It's Clytemnestra in you', and Electra soon comes to regret what she has done, much as in Euripides: 'I drove on, burning; your mind, reluctant metal, / I dipped it in fire and forged it sharp, day after day I beat and burned against you, and forged / A sword: I the arm'. Orestes abandons his sister, Argos and all human society. Jeffers concludes his dramatic poem with a Euripides-like dissolution of the house of Atreus: 'Electra turned and entered the ancient house. Orestes walked [away] in the clear dawn ... / ... climbed the tower beyond time ... and ... entered the earlier fountain'.[25]

After its first performance at the University of California in 1932, Jeffers adapted *The Tower beyond Tragedy* in 1941 for a fully staged production at the outdoor Forest Theatre near Jeffers' home in Carmel-by-the-Sea. The play had four performances, with the Australian-born British actress Judith Anderson as Clytemnestra. Encouraged by the response, Jeffers next adapted Euripides' *Medea*, with Judith Anderson in the title role, and the play was a smash hit on Broadway, running for six months from 1946–47. Jeffers brought *The Tower beyond Tragedy* to New York three years later, with Anderson again playing Clytemnestra. Drama critic Brooks Atkinson proclaimed Jeffers' poem on the Electra theme 'a masterpiece ... written in lines of fire that make an ancient theme seem immediate and devastating'. Of Anderson's performance, Atkinson wrote: 'No one should ever expect anything finer in the theater', adding that 'Marian Seldes' Electra and Alfred Ryder's Orestes ... keep the tragedy ominous and breathless after Clytemnestra has left it'.[26] Although focused on Clytemnestra, Robinson Jeffers' *The Tower beyond Tragedy* helped introduce Euripides' version of the Electra story to modern American audiences.

Long drawn to Greek tragedy, the American playwright Eugene O'Neill (1888–1953) began working on *Mourning Becomes Electra* three years after Jeffers published his dramatic poem. In an early entry in his work diary, O'Neill raised a question that guided his adaptation: 'Is it possible to get modern psychological approximation of Greek sense of fate ... which an intelligent audience of today, possessed of no belief in gods or supernatural retribution, could accept and be moved by?'[27] O'Neill identified the basic approach followed by almost every modern treatment of Greek tragedy since: character psychology is fate; the gods (and demons) are rooted within family histories and manifest in individual psyches; we hunt for the truth of others hidden behind the masks they wear; and we haunt our own selves by the masks we invent to hide our inmost fears from others. For O'Neill, tragic myths provided a framework for exploring the 'psychological fate' that afflicts modern man.

Mourning Becomes Electra relies heavily on the *Oresteia* – *The Homecoming, The Hunted, The Haunted* correspond to the three plays of Aeschylus's trilogy. But O'Neill also draws on Sophocles and Euripides' versions to explore the ill-fated Mannon house in the aftermath of the US Civil War. The decorated general Ezra Mannon returns from the front; his disaffected wife Christine and her lover Adam Brant arrange his death; the Mannon's daughter Lavinia discovers their affair and their role in her father's murder; fuelled with this knowledge, Lavinia's brother Orin kills Brant, whose murder drives their mother to suicide. Haunted by guilt over her death, Orin goes mad from 'the Furies within' and kills himself. Lavinia breaks off her engagement with Orin's friend Peter (the Pylades figure), and she withdraws into the desolate confines of the family home:

> Lavinia: There's no one left to punish me. I'm the last Mannon. I've got to punish myself! ... I'll live alone with the dead, and keep their secrets, and let them hound me, until the curse is paid out ... (*with a strange cruel smile of gloating over the years of self-torture*) ... It takes the Mannons to punish themselves for being born![28]

O'Neill considered Electra 'the most interesting of all women in drama'[29] and his Lavinia shares many traits with Euripides' heroine, as does Orin with Orestes. In psychoanalytic terms, the Mannon siblings display symptoms of the 'Oedipal' and the 'Electra complex'. Promoted by Sigmund Freud, the Oedipal complex assumes that a young boy sexually desires his mother, sees his father as competition which he cannot defeat, identifies with the male gender as he grows up, and his obsession turns away from its primal maternal source towards more suitable women. The 'Electra complex', developed by Freud's disciple Carl Jung, posits a comparable process for a young girl. She fights her mother for her father's affections until she realizes that she cannot win, then identifies with the female gender as she grows up and looks for men other than her father to fulfil her desires.[30]

Like Euripides' Electra (*El.* 1102–4), O'Neill's Lavinia prefers the patriarchal Ezra to the less than maternal Christine. However, she sees her mother as a rival not for her father, but for Adam Brant, to whom she is sexually attracted. Here O'Neill develops an idea implicit in Euripides – Electra's interest in Aegisthus's sexual life as her mother's 'kept man' (Eur. *El.* 945–49). For his part, Orin incestuously desires his mother and becomes murderously jealous when he learns of her affair with Brant. In terms of Euripides' *Electra*, we might compare Orestes' disgust that Clytemnestra and Aegisthus are breeding more children (*El.* 626), and his encouragement that Electra despoil Aegisthus's corpse (*El.* 896 – 9).

Resembling Orestes after the matricide, Orin is consumed with guilt following his mother's suicide. He then tries to transfer his sexual desire to his sister, but Lavinia rejects his overtures, and Orin kills himself. Lavinia soldiers on by shutting herself up in the accursed house of the Mannons, alone with the ghosts and the memories. In his *Electra*, Euripides challenges the ancient myth of heroic vengeance; in *Mourning Becomes Electra*, O'Neill embraces the modern myth of family-bred psychological fate.

For all of its impact on American drama, Greek tragedy has exerted far greater influence on French theatre and culture. From the Late Renaissance onwards, French artists, composers, and playwrights have turned to tragic myth for inspiration – the operas of Lully, Charpentier, Rameau, Gluck, Berlioz, and Offenbach; the neoclassical tragedies of Corneille, Racine, Voltaire, and Crébillon (his *Électre* appeared in 1709); and later adaptations by Giraudoux, Cocteau, Anouilh, and Sartre. In

1937, Jean Giraudoux (1882–1944) produced his *Électre*, the first French play in centuries with a strong connection to Euripides' *Electra*.[31]

A drama of striking originality, Giraudoux's *Électre* draws on Aeschylus and Sophocles, but owes its biggest classical debt to Euripides. Égisthe tries to marry off Électre to the palace gardener; the young woman hates her mother and drives the reluctant Oreste to murder; the intractable relationship between mythic inheritance and individual choice remains problematic until the end. A similar issue arises in Euripides' tragedy, whose heroine clings to an unreal vision of her heroic brother, and to an unquestioning sense of the justice of matricidal revenge. These articles of faith shatter with Electra's horror at what she and Orestes have done. In Giraudoux's version, however, Électre remains unwavering in her commitment to righting perceived wrongs until the bitter end.

Like Euripides, Giraudoux incorporates ironic twists and comic elements that unsettle the tragic mood, yet paradoxically raise the dramatic stakes.[32] He introduces a small 'Chorus' of Eumenides ('kindly spirits'), the name given to the chthonic forces of vengeance when they are transformed at the end of Aeschylus's *Oresteia*. Young girls at the start of the play, they predict that Électre 'is going to poison everything with her venom … of truth, the only one without an antidote.'[33] When she drives her brother to matricide, they rage at her for forcing them to 'mature' into their old roles as Furies who must hound Oreste to madness.

Already committed to punishing her mother, Électre belatedly discovers that Égisthe and Clytemnestre killed Agamemnon. She now justifies her life-long loathing of her mother by claiming that she serves an impartial cosmic justice that abides no exceptions.[34] Électre applies the same law to Égisthe, even though he transforms over the play from a petty tyrant to the only leader that can defend Argos against a foreign invasion. In Électre's absolutist view, Oreste must kill Clytemnestre and Égisthe, even though it means the annihilation of Argos. The drama ends with the city burned to the ground, while Électre's sense of justice remains intact. Euripides leaves the city of Argos abandoned; Giraudoux leaves it destroyed.

Giraudoux re-imagines Euripides' *Electra* as a tangle of lies and deceptions that lead to disaster – lies about the past, about personal motivation, about justice, about purity, about love, about privilege and social class. Although he denies his Électre repentance or regret, Giraudoux ends his play very much as Euripides does. Argos loses its leaders; Aegisthus and Clytemnestra lie dead; Orestes and Electra are banished. Writing in 1937, when Europe feared the return of cataclysmic violence, Giraudoux delivered a tragedy that was not fated to be one. In so doing, he tapped a strong undercurrent in Euripides' original.[35]

Seven years after the premiere of Giraudoux's play, the Belgian-born novelist and playwright Marguerite Yourcenar (1903–1987) began *Électre, ou La chute des masques* (*Electra, or the Fall of the Masks*).[36] In her foreword to the published text, Yourcenar explains why she chose Euripides' tragedy as her model: 'His play corresponded to the taste and the conditions of our time ... I went to the most somber realist, whose protagonists – hidden away or on the run – are accustomed to an underground way of life, where poverty and humiliation make their hatred venomous'.[37]

Forced into marriage with the farmer Théodore, Yourcenar's Électre lives on bitterness and hatred. Her motivation for vengeance stems from loss of status; the need to punish her father's slayers plays a relatively minor role. Like Euripides' farmer, Théodore honours his wife (and her virginity), even though their fundamental values differ. Bound to the land, Théodore views the natural cycle as worthy of respect and wonder, and the etymology of his name – 'gift of god' – indicates his decent character. Électre, however, sees nature as a tool she can turn to her own ends: 'I had my own seasons ... my poisoned fruit ripening on secret vines'. To have a baby would interfere with her 'brainchild': 'Isn't this murder our child? ... Aren't the odds that I will die of it, covered with blood as though I had given birth'.[38] The parallels with Euripides' play are striking.

Reflecting her protagonist's preference for mental rather than natural fertility, Yourcenar sets the action inside, within the four walls of Théodore's dirt-floor cottage.[39] Nature, as it were, is kept at bay. Électre lures Clytemnestre from the palace with the ruse of a newborn child, and she arrives (like Euripides' Old Man) with a basket of food. Instead of a meal, however, an angry exchange ensues between mother and daughter. Debunking Électre's idealized view of her father, Clytemnestre portrays Agamemnon as a brutal conqueror and ruthless colonizer (shades of Hitler and Mussolini enter into her depiction).

Describing how the teenage Électre flirted with Égisthe, provocatively allowing a glimpse of her shoulder and leg, Clytemnestre forces her daughter to admit her sexual attraction to him. Both ashamed and jealous, Électre cannot forgive her mother for taking Égisthe as her husband and leaving her a miserable marriage with a poor farmer. In Euripides' play, Electra holds onto Orestes' sword when he drives it into his mother (Eur. *El.* 1225); Yourcenar has Électre kill Clytemnestre by herself, with her own two hands.

A confrontation between Oreste and Égisthe balances the deadly encounter between mother and daughter. Learning of Clytemnestre's murder, Égisthe informs the young man of the family secret – he, and not Agamemnon, is Oreste's real father. Filled from childhood with stories of his warrior father Agamemnon, Oreste cannot endure the truth: 'So I cried for the wrong father since the age of twelve!'[40] When Égisthe expresses unconditional love for his son, the enraged Orestes stabs him. The dying Égisthe instructs his guards to let Électre, Oreste, and Pylades leave; he refuses to implicate them in his assassination.

As the subtitle *La chute des masques* ('The Fall of the Masks') indicates, Yourcenar's version of the Electra story – much like Giraudoux's – consists of a web of deception and lies: by Clytemnestre and Égisthe to their son Oreste; by Oreste to himself, preferring a mythologized Agamemnon to his real father; by Pylade to Oreste, pretending to be a friend while serving as an agent for Égisthe and by Pylade to Égisthe, whom he betrays by helping Oreste with the murder; by Électre to her mother, inventing a newborn baby, and to herself by never admitting her attraction to Égisthe. The most distressing deception involves the character of Théodore. When he returns from the fields, he is arrested as the party responsible for the murders of Égisthe and Clytemnestre.

Électre has escaped with Pylade and Oreste, but Théodore remains ever loyal. He delivers the closing lines of the play: 'The angels have accomplished their butcher's task ... I know everything. Nothing occurred without me. I am Electra's husband'.[41]

Like other French writers at the time, Yourcenar turned to Greek tragedy for the strength to keep writing in the face of Nazi terror and the hypocrisy of the Vichy government. Championing patriotic compromise for the good of France, Marshal Pétain and most of the country accepted the Nazi occupation and more or less did their oppressor's bidding. Confronting the hollow myth of national honour, Yourcenar found Euripides' *Electra* all too relevant. With twisted killers and a phantom Helen, Euripides' play presented a world that desperately wanted to believe in the past, in its heroes, and in the narratives that supported them. Like Euripides, Yourcenar dared to expose how misplaced – and dangerous – such faith had become.

In 1962, Cypriot-born Michael Cacoyannis made a signal contribution to the reception of Euripides' *Electra* with the first film in what became his Trojan trilogy.[42] Shot in black and white on location in ancient Mycenae, *Elektra* closely follows Euripides' plot, adding a 'prequel' to help modern audiences with the background story. Cacoyannis opens the film with scenes from Aeschylus's *Agamemnon*: the king's triumphal return from the Trojan War, Clytemnestra's extravagant welcome, and Agamemnon's murder (along with Cassandra) in the bath, their death cries echoing off the cold stone walls. The film then moves ahead several years to Electra's forced marriage to the peasant farmer, her loss of status captured in the long trip on a donkey cart from the palace to the impoverished farmhouse (see Figure 6).

The film gives a realistic sense of hardscrabble country life, with a group of peasant women replacing the eager maidens of Euripides' Chorus (see Figure 4). The setting emphasizes the wrongs done to Electra, whose unquenchable hatred is etched into memory by the searing performance of Irene Pappas in the title role. We meet a young (but not self-conscious) Orestes, who returns incognito with Pylades; a vicious Aegisthus, cruel and drunk (his sacrifice and banquet to the nymphs resembles a Dionysian orgy); a deeply vain Clytemnestra, whose arrival at the cottage conveys the vastly different worlds of the queen with her Trojan slaves, and the daughter with her village women (see Figure 3). The carefully calibrated score by Mikis Theodorakis never succumbs to Hollywood overkill, remaining sombre and spare until the murders. Sharp staccatos and rising pitch accompany the violence, which are filmed, not narrated, but eschew blood and gore. No gods appear at the end.

Consistent with the setting, a cinematic realism defines the film, which leads Cacoyannis to iron out (or eliminate) the elements that make Euripides' play so challenging: the ironic, occasionally comic tone; the self-dramatization of the main characters; the gap between heroic idealization and mundane reality; the doubts about the oracle and the role of the gods. In place of the Dioskouroi, the film closes with the villagers silhouetted in silence against the landscape, ominous and disapproving of those who brought bloodshed to their community. The privileged aristocrats must leave, or (one suspects) they will be driven out. Pylades and Elektra depart for their life together; in the opposite direction Orestes makes his way towards Athens for his trial and eventual purification. The Greek villagers remain, as stern and timeless as the Argive hills that loom behind them, bearing witness to a tragedy that seems as inevitable as the earth and the sky.

These different productions and adaptations of *Electra* capture something of the range of artistic and cultural responses to Euripides' play, but barely cover the waterfront. Elements from Euripides' *Electra* find their way into poems by H.D. (Hilda Doolittle, 'A Dead Priestess Speaks'), Sylvia Plath ('Daddy', 'Azalea Path'), and Marilyn Hacker ('Elektra on Third Avenue', 'For Elektra'), and into novels by Thomas Berger (*Orrie's Story*), Joyce Carol Oates (*Angel of Light*), and Colm Tóibín (*House of Names*).

Wherever traces of Euripides' play may be found, they have a way of pointing us back to the original. I think you will find there, as I have done, a complex, disturbing, and deeply compelling play. At one with the genre of 'Greek tragedy', Euripides' *Electra* also complicates what we think we mean when we employ that time-honoured term.

Notes

Introduction

1   Emily Vermeule (1959), Philip Vellacott (1963), Janet Lembke and
    Kenneth Reckford (1994), James Morwood (1997), and Elizabeth Seydel
    Morgan (1998). In 1980, playwright Adrienne Kennedy adapted *Electra*
    and *Orestes* for a production at the Juilliard School. This powerful
    cut-down version follows Euripides' *Electra* very closely, but it eliminates
    the Farmer prologue (replaced by the Chorus), Orestes' speech on
    nobility, and the appearance of Castor and Polydeuces at the end
    (Kennedy 2001).
2   All dates are BC (unless otherwise noted), except in the last chapter dealing
    with later productions and adaptations of *Electra*. The Greek text referred
    to is Kovacs (1998), supplemented by Cropp (2013) and Roisman and
    Luschnig (2011). Translations are my own, although I draw heavily on
    Kovacs (1998). Spelling and transliteration follow popular practice and
    aim for ease of recognition. Endnotes with author, date, and page numbers
    refer to entries in the References; in the notes, I use cf. in the sense of
    'contrast'.

Chapter 1

1   Some scholars believe women could not attend the theatre; however, cults
    and festivals linked to Dionysus generally were open to women (Rehm
    2002, 322 n.94). On the complex question of the 'competence' of ancient
    audiences, see Revermann (2006).
2   On ancient play production, see Rehm (2017, 13–33), Csapo (2007),
    Wilson (2000), and Csapo and Slater (1995).
3   For the survival of Greek tragic texts, including Euripides' *Electra*, see
    Chapter 9.
4   The current remains of the theatre of Dionysus date from the first to the
    third centuries AD, some 500–700 years after Euripides' *Electra*. Visiting the

theatre now, one must think away the stone seats, the paved semi-circular orchestra, the stone stage (*proskênê*, 'proscenium'), and the built-up modern city of Athens sprawling into the distance. The earliest permanent (stone) foundations in the theatre date from the fourth century BC, and archaeologists have found no substantive evidence for the oft-repeated claim that the original shape of the *orchêstra* was circular. Until the building of the theatre at Epidaurus a century after Euripides' death, no Greek theatre had a circular playing area or used such a template for theatre construction. See Rehm (2017, 34–50); also Papastamati-Von Moock (2015), Csapo (2007), and Moretti (1999–2000).

5 Some think that the corpses were carried out through the central door, mirroring the removal of Aegisthus's corpse from the *orchêstra* into the cottage earlier in the play. It seems more likely that Euripides mirrored the staging in Aeschylus's *Oresteia*, which used the *ekkuklêma* to reveal the corpses of Agamemnon and Cassandra in *Agamemnon*, and those of Clytemnestra and Aegisthus in *Choepori* (discussed in Chapter 3).

6 Mastronarde (1990); more generally Dunn (1996). Nine of Euripides' eighteen surviving plays (few now attribute *Rhesus* to Euripides) feature the arrival of a god or gods on high near the end of the play. If one counts the appearance of Medea in the chariot of Helios, Euripides ends ten of his tragedies with a *deus* entry. Gods also appear on high at the start of *Trojan Women* and arrive unexpectedly in the middle of *Heracles* to strike the hero mad.

7 The performers in the dithyrambic competitions at Athens did not wear masks, but actors and choruses in tragedy and comedy always did.

8 Drawing on M.M. Bakhtin (*The Dialogic Imagination: Four Essays* [1981], Austin: University of Texas Press, 130–46), Csapo (2002, 139–40) points out that modern realism 'strives to reveal character inwardly as a private and unique essence. But . . . the ancients generally constructed character outwardly as a public persona defined by a broad typology oriented less to psychological than to sociological distinctions that define one's *état civil*'. This outside-in approach helps explain how ancient actors could play multiple roles in the same play, often in quick succession.

9 The Farmer uses the normal spoken metre in tragedy, iambic trimeter (three metrical 'feet', each consisting of an unstressed-stressed, unstressed-stressed pattern, with some variants), what we would call iambic hexameter: six iambic feet, alternating unstressed and stressed

syllables. Shakespeare uses a similar form with five metrical feet, iambic
pentameter ('blank verse'), as in Portia's lines from *The Merchant of Venice*:
'The **qual** / **ity**/ of **mer**/cy **is**/ not **strained**'. On Greek metre generally, see
West (1987); for metre in *Electra*, Cropp (2013) and Roisman and
Luschnig (2011) provide scansion and commentary.

10 Sifakis (2002, 161 n.33).

11 Aimed to reach out to its audience, Greek tragedy features 'language
fledged for flight' (Tony Harrison, 'A Poet's Drama,' lecture at Getty
Museum conference, 'Contemporary Performance of Greek and
Roman Drama', 20 June 2002). In the view of actress Fiona Shaw
(2010, xi), 'A poetic scale of performance makes the actor rise and meet
the language with the spatiality of a stage that does not mimic the
domestic'.

12 The Orestes actor also may have played the Messenger who announces
Orestes' victory over Aegisthus (Cropp 2013, 13–14; Dickin 2009, 131; cf.
Marshall 1999–2000, 337–40). However, only twenty-one lines separate
the Messenger's exit from Orestes' entrance, making for a very quick
change.

13 I use 'Chorus' for the performers (understood as a plural entity), 'chorus'
for the lyric that they perform. See Gould (1996), Goldhill (1996), Foley
(2003), and Rehm (2017, 59–69) on the various functions of the tragic
Chorus.

14 In only five extant tragedies does the Chorus leave the stage and return
later: Aeschylus's *Eumenides*, Sophocles' *Ajax*, Euripides' *Alcestis* and
Helen, and the fourth-century *Rhesus*. Euripides plays with this possibility
in *Electra* when, at the sight of strange men (Orestes and Pylades), Electra
tells the Chorus to flee 'down the track' while she runs into the cottage (*El.*
215–19). Assurances from the (disguised) Orestes keep either departure
from taking place; see Arnott (1973, 53–54).

15 At one point the Chorus of *Electra* actually refer to this accompaniment
(*El.* 435), calling attention to their own role as performers in the play.
Euripides uses this technique (discussed further in Chapters 4 and 8) to
encourage the audience to think about how the story gets told.

16 Born in 480 BC, either on the island of Salamis or in the Athenian *deme*
(*dêmos*, 'borough') of Phylla, Euripides died in Macedonia in 406. No one
knows why he left Athens near the end of his life for the court of Archelaus
in northern Greece, but he did present a tragedy there (*Archelaus*, named

for the ruler's ancestor). On Euripides' ancient biography (much of it suspect), see Scodel (2017) and Lefkowitz (2012, 87–103). Ancient sources credit Euripides with some ninety-five plays.

17 Dickin (2009, 53–86); more generally, de Jong (1991) and Barrett (2002).

18 Zeitlin (1970) examines the role of Hera and the Argive Heraion in the play. Electra refuses to participate in the festival dance of brides-to-be, even as she joins the lyric of her friends, an irony that accentuates the difference between her and the Chorus (Weiss 2018, 69–73).

19 For the *aulos* used for marching, rowing, and other activities, see West (1992, 28–30); also Csapo (1999).

20 A formal debate (*agôn*) occurs frequently in Euripides (Lloyd 1992, esp. 1–36, 55–70; Collard 1975). In *Electra*, he uses fifth-century Athenian legal language for the punishment of Aegisthus and Clytemnestra (*El.* 484, 668, 953). See Kells (1966) and Cropp (2013, on 668).

Chapter 2

1 Aristotle, *Poetics* 1450a 15–16; Golden and Hardison (1981, 13 and 127–31).

2 I avoid the word 'act' because of its associations with later European drama, structured around the rise and fall of a curtain, or a series of blackouts, marking the beginning and end of each section. Greek tragedy does not share in this convention and is not constructed in this way.

3 The manuscripts and papyrus fragments show no such divisions, only the metrical shifts from dialogue to lyric metre, and an occasional mark to indicate the change of speaker (rarely named, requiring editors to assign speakers from the context). The folios and quartos of Shakespeare also indicate no act or scene breaks. Modern editors have invented these tools to help find specific scenes and passages in the text.

4 Brecht (2015, 109–10, 117, 122–25).

5 These time indicators do not imply that performances at the City Dionysia began at sunrise, a practical impossibility given the size of the audience, the performers' preparation, the logistics of animal wrangling, the pre-performance ceremonies, etc.

6 Tracking servants across the play requires care. Some think Electra has a servant, pointing to the lines 'Take this jug off my head' (*El.* 140), but the Scholiast (an anonymous ancient commentator) has it right: 'Electra says this to herself' (Roisman and Luschnig 2011, on 140). Two servants accompany Orestes and Pylades on their initial entrance; the Farmer addresses them at 360–61. One of these returns as the Messenger, a speaking part played either by the Orestes' actor wearing the servant's mask, or the actor who played the Farmer and the Old Man. The latter actor returns as Clytemnestra, and then later as Castor. Two servants bring on the body of Aegisthus, one of Orestes' original servants and another mute actor, perhaps understood to be one of Aegisthus's men who now supports Orestes (851–53). When ordered by Orestes (959–61), they take Aegisthus's body offstage, probably accompanied by Pylades. We are meant to forget their presence in the cottage during the matricide, one of many examples of tragedy's disinterest in strict dramatic realism.

7 This is most likely the great Argive Heraia, celebrated every four years in the spring. The Heraia festival featured games and ritual ploughing with a team of oxen, an act associated with fertility, both agricultural and human. The practice also refers to the festival's foundation in honour of Kleobis and Biton, the dutiful sons of the priestess of Hera (Herodotus 1.31). When oxen could not be found, they yoked themselves to their mother's cart and pulled her six miles to arrive at the festival on time. The priestess prayed to Hera to bestow on her sons the greatest of gifts, and her wish was granted: their deaths. The irony seems inescapable – in *Electra*, the children bestow that 'gift' on their mother.

8 By moving from lyric into dialogue metre, Euripides uses the two lines of the Chorus and two lines of Electra, to mark a shift in the action, back (as it were) to the plot.

9 The exchange between Orestes and Electra runs seventy lines. Euripides goes further in his *Ion*, when a long-separated mother and son share over one hundred lines of *stichomythia* (the longest such passage in tragedy), with no recognition at the end.

10 Electra's speech features a high number of resolutions (irregularities in the normal dialogue metre), indicating her agitation (Roisman and Luschnig 2011, on 300–38).

11 The Chorus do not describe the famous shield forged by Hephaestus in
   Iliad 18, but the armour presented to the young Achilles before he sets off
   for Troy.

12 Here Euripides parodies the recognition scene from Aeschylus's *Choephori*,
   discussed in Chapter 3.

13 'In this the shortest of all recognition scenes [in tragedy], no terms of
   endearment, no personal appellations are exchanged' (Hartigan 1991,
   114).

14 Electra uses a beacon image a hundred lines later for news of Orestes'
   encounter with Aegisthus, perhaps a reference to Clytemnestra's 'fire
   speech' in Aeschylus's *Agamemnon* (Roisman and Luschnig 2011, on
   585–89).

15 Electra's interruption of the rapid dialogue between Orestes and the Old
   Man demonstrates her 'take-charge' attitude *vis-à-vis* the matricide.

16 'In the three tragedians there are twenty-six messengers and heralds who
   enter a play to give extended information. This is the only one not trusted
   on sight' (Gellie 1981, 4). Arnott (1973, 50–53) shrewdly analyses this and
   other 'red-herrings' in the play.

17 Orestes may have cut off Aegisthus's head, a possibility dealt with in detail
   in Chapter 6.

18 The father of Pelops (and great-grandfather of Agamemnon), Tantalus was
   a mortal son of Zeus. He offended the gods so greatly (the exact crime
   remains unclear) that after his death they condemned him to eternal
   punishment in Hades, where he was 'tantalized' with food and drink that
   always remained just out of reach.

19 Not named here (or by Euripides in *Orestes* 1645–46), the town was
   Orestheion, located near the source of the Alpheus river, which also flows
   through Olympia (*El.* 781–82). See Thucydides 5.6.34 and Herodotus 9.11.

Chapter 3

1 The fact that Greek tragedies reiterate earlier versions of the myth and
  accept their basic structure suggests to some that the genre demonstrates
  the impossibility of social and political progress. 'The whole drama is
  "scarred," both made and marred by its inescapable relations to anterior

texts' (Goff 1991, 261). For Wohl (2015, 87), '*Electra* suggests that tragic form, far from instantiating a "utopian tendency," instead smothers it'. Artistic form and content are indeed intertwined; however, common sense tells us that the shape of the bottle does not necessarily determine its contents.

2   Garvie (1988, ix–xxvi, 'The Story before Aeschylus') provides a thorough account; also Cropp (2013, 20–31), March (1987, 79–118, focusing on Clytemnestra), and Swift (2015).

3   Euripides' *Electra* incorporates several elements from Homer's *Odyssey*. The Farmer's hut and his welcome recall the hospitality shown by the swineherd Eumaeus to Odysseus (disguised as a beggar); Orestes' scar brings to mind the lesion that betrays Odysseus's identity to his old nurse Eurykleia (H. *Od.* 19.388–475); the drunk, lascivious Aegisthus (Eur. *El.* 326–31) conjures up the suitors on Ithaca; Orestes' murder of Aegisthus at a feast reverses Aegisthus's murder of Agamemnon at a welcoming banquet (H. *Od.* 11.409–15). See Davidson (1999–2000, 120–22), Goff (1991), Michelini (1987, 185–86), Cropp (1986, 189–96), and Tarkow (1981). Neither the character of Electra nor the murder of Clytemnestra appears in the Homeric account.

4   The Epic Cycle (Davies 1989); Xanthus's and Stesichorus's *Oresteia*'s (Campbell 1991, 26–27, 127–33). On the genesis of 'Electra' as the name of Agamemnon and Clytemnestra's younger daughter, see Moreau (1984, esp. 64–78).

5   Prag 1985. Scholars reasonably assume that a revival of Aeschylus's *Oresteia* occurred in Athens around 425 BC. See Marshall (2017, 46–52, drawing on Ar. *Acharnians* 9–11 and Ar. *Frogs* 868–69) and Hammond (1984, 386–87, referring to vase paintings); cf. Biles (2006–7). On fifth-century re-performances of Aeschylus generally, see Lamari (2017, 18, 58–77).

6   Which of the two *Electra*'s came first remains in doubt. For Finglass (2007, 2), the uncertainty of dating Sophocles' *Electra* precludes 'even a provisional decision' on priority, and Cropp (2013, 26–28, 31–33) concurs. Based on resolutions in the iambic trimeter line, some argue that Euripides' play likely came first (Lloyd 2005, 17–18, 31; March 2001, 20–22 and 1987, 115–16; Harder 1995, 15). Others think Sophocles' tragedy is probably earlier (Roisman and Luschnig 2011, 30–32; Michelini 1987, 185–87, 199–202; Bernard 1985, 245–46; Conacher 1967, 202–3, n.9;

Denniston 1939, xxxiv–xxxix). Without direct evidence, even metrical dating is problematic – out of 120 plays by Sophocles, merely seven survive intact; out of roughly ninety-five by Euripides, only eighteen are extant.

7 Cropp (2013 on 518–44) summarizes the various opinions on Euripides' use of Aeschylus's recognition scene, with extensive bibliography. See also Roisman and Luschnig (2011 on 522–44), Ronnet (1975), and Torrance (2011).

8 Euripides refers to this scene again in *Orestes* (408 BC). Electra asks her ailing brother, 'Would you like me to set your feet on the ground? / It's a long time since you made a footprint' (Eur. *Or.* 233 –34; see Wright 2008, 121).

9 Onstage with Orestes for some two hundred lines, Electra fails to notice the scar; she only sees it when the Old Man points it out. Unlike Odysseus, whose scar came from a wild boar during a dangerous hunt (above n.3), Orestes fell when chasing a pet deer, a most unheroic adventure (Tarkow 1981, 144; Goff 1991, 260). For a comparison of the recognition of Orestes in Aeschylus, Sophocles, and Euripides, see McClure (2015, 219–29) and Zeitlin (2012).

10 von Schlegel (1815, 235) saw Euripides as 'the precursor of the new comedy', an idea developed in a seminal article by Knox (1979). In the recognition scene, 'the comic rudely interjects itself into the tragic mode' (Michelini 1987, 206); the country setting 'confère á la pièce une tonalité très pariculière' (Bernard 1985, 248); the domestic feel of the Farmer/ Electra exchanges suggests an 'assimilation of the comic universe' (Michelini 1987, 100); the play shows Euripides' penchant 'for making sophisticated jokes at the expense of gods, of Aeschylus, and of stage conventions' (Winnington-Ingram 1969, 132; also Gellie 1981; Goff 1999–2000). For all of Euripides' experiments with comic and parodic tonalities, Mastronarde (1999–2000) rightly insists that the ancient genre of tragedy had no trouble encompassing them. After all, Aristotle refers to Euripides as 'the most tragic' of the playwrights (*Poetics* 1453a 30).

11 In Aeschylus and Sophocles, Orestes must insinuate himself into the palace. Euripides, however, turns this problem inside out, for Orestes 'has to bring the victim to the killers' (Carey 2008, 96).

12 As Halporn (1983, 114) puts it, 'At the end of the play there is a tie of blood between Electra and Orestes; it is not the blood of the father in their veins, but the blood of the mother on their hands'. Segal (1985, 22) emphasizes

the 'atmosphere of internal doubt, guilt, self-pollution, and self-disgust' that differentiates the matricide in Euripides from those in Aeschylus and Sophocles.

13 At line 360 the Farmer tells Orestes' servants to bring his belongings inside, but Orestes and his entourage don't enter until line 400. Perhaps the servants look for a sign from their master that they must enter the hovel; Orestes responds with a speech explaining indirectly why they should swallow their pride. Denniston (1939 on 396–98) finds Orestes' tone 'a little ungracious. His enthusiasm for the noble Farmer seems to have cooled'.

14 Vernant (1972, 285).

15 The word occurs some twenty-three times, often with great emphasis. After the matricide, Orestes returns to the stage crying out, 'O Earth [*Ga*] and Zeus who sees all / mortal acts, look on this deed of bloodshed / and pollution . . .' (Eur. *El.* 1177–79). Another word for 'ground', *chthôn*, occurs eight times in the play. Castor's uses it for the chasm at the base of the Areopagus where the city will establish a cult for the Furies (1271), again linking the end of *Electra* to that of Aeschylus's *Eumenides*.

16 In his *Trojan Women*, Euripides employs a similar phrase for the end of the war, *dekasporôi chronôi* (20), literally 'in the tenth-sowing year'.

17 Built on reciprocity of giving and receiving, Greek religion depended on animal sacrifice, which also provided meat for human consumption – only the fat of the victims was offered to the gods. At the Argive Heraia, to which the Chorus invite Electra, a hundred oxen were sacrificed, giving the festival its popular name, *Hekatombaia* ('one-hundred bulls').

18 For a summary of the dating controversy, see Roisman and Luschnig (2011, 28–32); also Cropp (2013, 25–28, and on 998–1123).

19 Both Sophocles' funerary urn and Euripides' water jug may have reminded audiences of the ritual vessels brought by Electra and the Chorus in Aeschylus's *Choephoroi*. In Euripides, however, Electra's prop serves only pragmatic needs. See Hammond (1984, 378–81), Luschnig (1995, 89–93), Easterling (1997, 168–69), and Stieber (2009, 249–50).

Chapter 4

1 Grube (1941, 314).

2   Aristotle, *Poetics* 1450b 27–33; Golden and Hardison (1981, 14 and 139–42).

3   Some 'performance studies' theorists argue that performance informs every aspect of human life; a performance that appears to end simply morphs into another performance, *ad infinitum*, or *ad nauseam*, depending on whether this process takes us deeper into the world, or keeps us circulating endlessly on its surface; see R. Rehm (2003), *Radical Theatre: Greek Tragedy and the Modern World*, London: Duckworth, 9–16.

4   Stieber (2009).

5   Goldhill (1986a, 163).

6   Michelini (1987, 187) considers *eugenia* ('nobility', 'good-breeding') the major theme of *Electra*.

7   His prologue has 'the longest delay before identification [of the speaker] of any extant Euripidean play' (Hartigan 1991, 108 n.6).

8   Because the Greeks valued financial independence, 'the man who farms his own land is his own man, unlike the craftsman, the market trader or the hired hand … for Euripides the character of the farmer came loaded with ideological implications' (Carey 2008, 101). See Burford (1993, 167–72) on the positive valence of land-based independence in ancient Greece; also Denniston (1939, on 253, and on 367–72) and Blaicklock (1952, 175–76).

9   Vermeule (1959, 3) refers to the 'double vision' at work in the play: 'Electra's image of the truth, and the truth itself, stubbornly refuse to match'. Luschnig (1995, 109) agrees: 'Sadly no one really lives up to her vision and she must invent a self and the other characters who will play the roles suitable to her tragedy'. Hartigan (1991, 122) writes that 'Elektra sees a glorious avenger, a tomb-desecrating usurper, a gleefully luxuriating and coldhearted queen … But … Euripides has presented us with a cowardly Orestes, a genial, if unhappy, Aigisthos, a self-deprecating somewhat motherly Klytaimnestra'. For similar views on Electra, see Burian (1997, 180), Tarkow (1981, 150–51), Arnott (1981, 185–86), Conacher (1967, 204–10), O'Brien (1964, 36), Adams (1935), England (1926), and Sheppard (1918). Those who interpret Electra more sympathetically include Ringer (2016, 147–56), Lloyd (1986, 1–10), Zeitlin (1970, 647–51), and Bates (1930, 89), who sees Electra as 'a young woman of a gentle nature who has been deeply wronged by her mother'. For a useful comparison of Euripides and Sophocles' portrayal of their title character, see Harder (1995).

10 Michelini (1987, 209), Conacher (1967, 208), Grube (1941, 300–3).

11 Denniston (1939, on 71–73). Barlow (2008, 54) calls attention to Electra's 'self-conscious . . . romantic posturing', as do many others.

12 Something similar occurs in Euripides' *Bacchae* (215–48). Pentheus enters and delivers a tirade against the Theban maenads, failing to notice the presence of Cadmus and Teiresias, already onstage for forty-five lines.

13 'Electra feels her poverty more now because it can be seen by others' (Roisman and Luschnig 2011, on 403–31).

14 'Fear has infected all the major characters to a degree unknown in the corresponding plays by Aeschylus and Sophocles' (O'Brien 1964, 18). Aegisthus is so characterized (Eur. *El.* 22–23, 25–26, 39, 617, 831–35), as is Orestes (336–38, 982), Clytemnestra (30, 643, 1114), and Electra (216–21, 686–92, 695–98, 757–59, 911–12).

15 Electra asks her mother, 'Why, after killing your husband didn't you / hand over the ancestral home to us?' (*El.* 1088–89). As Conacher (1967, 208) puts it, 'She is vexed to the point of murder by the loss of her patrimony'. See more generally Griffin (2008).

16 On Electra's sudden change, von Schlegel (1815, 172) thinks that her 'repentance . . . arises from no moral feeling, but merely from a commotion of the senses'. Cf. Walsh (1977, 286): 'Electra blames herself . . . and rightly, because she knows best that she killed Clytemnestra not because Apollo demanded it, but because she desired it herself'.

17 In *Hecuba*, *Trojan Women*, and *Ion*, Euripides also has a character sing a monody before the Chorus's *parodos*, but only Electra performs a strophic song, as if playing both parts in a call-and-response dirge (Roisman and Luschnig 2011, on 112–13; also on 125 and 140).

18 These differences may reflect their relative ages. In this play, Orestes seems the younger, as he does in Euripides' *Orestes*, but not in his *Iphigeneia in Aulis* (Roisman and Luschnig 2011, 254–55).

19 'The young Argive aristocrat convicts himself out of his own mouth' (Adams 1935, 120); 'a talker and a *poseur*, he dramatises himself' (Blaicklock 1952, 168); Orestes is 'the touchstone that proves the case' (Hartigan 1991, 110); 'The failure of Orestes to realize the applicability of these arguments to his own behaviour and noble birth offers a typically Euripidean sardonic comment on the distance between words and the world' (Goldhill 1986, 228–29).

20 Roisman and Luschnig (2011, on 671–84).

21 The noun that Orestes applies to the oracle, *amathia*, has many meanings – 'senselessness', 'stupidity', 'ignorance', 'foolishness', 'lack of inner feeling' – all of which fit the context.

22 Electra shames Aegisthus in similar fashion: 'I don't like girlish men, but ones who are manly' (*andreiou*, 949). When she calls Orestes a coward, she uses the term 'un-manly' (*anandrian*, 982).

23 Moreau (1984, 76) sees Pylades as Orestes' 'double', because Electra greets him as her brother's equal following Aegisthus's murder. However, Electra expresses no excitement or interest in her imminent union with Pylades at the end of the play.

24 Female Choruses sympathetic to the heroine appear often in Euripides; of eighteen extant plays, only four (*Heracles*, *Children of Heracles*, *Alcestis*, *Cyclops*) have a male Chorus.

25 Electra's word-choice sounds forced; the Chorus live far from city, with little knowledge of what goes on there (*El.* 298–99). They learn of the upcoming festival in Argos from a mountain dweller from Mycenae, who spread the news to the hinterland (169–74).

26 These choruses employ 'New Music', a lyric style popular in Athens towards the end of the fifth century. These songs value word pictures over structure, and sensual detail over logical narrative. They feature compound adjectives full of colour and sound, and adopt a singing style called 'melism', where a syllable might extend over several notes (Csapo 2003, esp. 71–74, 94–95; also Cropp 2013, on 432–86; and Csapo 1999–2000). For useful readings of the first *stasimon*, emphasizing the change from idyllic heroism to grisly violence, see Csapo (2009), Morwood (1981), King (1980), and Walsh (1977). According to Walsh (1977, 278), 'the contrast between ode and what precedes it produces something like *Verfremdungseffekt*' (Bertolt Brecht's term for 'distancing' or 'making strange'). Brecht developed this technique to keep the audience alert to the manner of the story's unfolding, preventing them from abandoning their critical judgement to the momentum of the plot, and from losing themselves in sentimental sympathy with the characters (Brecht 2015, 101–8, 143–46, 166–67, 181–98, 241–42, 251–54).

27 The Chorus's change is 'partly an echo of the inconsistency that Euripides builds into his tragic world, and partly a traditional privilege of the chorus position . . ., serving both intradramatic and extradramatic goals' (Mastronarde 2010, 121; also Foley 2003).

28 The Greeks called the dolphin's blowhole an *aulos*, associating the mammal's breathing to a kind of sea-music (Aristotle, *History of Animals*, 537a-b).

29 The repetition (at *El.* 503, 524, 553, 566, 570, 577, 598, 618, 651, 664) drives the point home. Old people feature prominently in Euripides' tragedies: the Chorus in *Heracles*, Iolaus in *Children of Heracles*, Peleus in *Andromache*, the aged veteran in *Iphigenia in Aulis*, Creusa's Tutor in *Ion*. Although not decrepit, Hecuba (*Hecuba, Trojan Women*), Iphis (*Suppliant Women*), Jocasta (*Phoenician Women*), Pheres (*Alcestis*), and Silenus (*Cyclops*) all speak of the difficulties of old age.

30 The Old Man unconsciously echoes Electra's line to Orestes: 'Once I have shed my mother's blood, then let me die' (281).

31 The Tutor in *Ion*, the Old Man in *Iphigenia in Aulis*, and Iolaus in *Children of Heracles* also find their strength restored by a new mission (murder plot, a letter to deliver, an impending battle).

32 Often in tragedy, the actor playing the Messenger will narrate the suffering of a character he played earlier, and the Orestes actor could have played the Messenger (Chapter 1, note 12). If so, Electra would fail to recognize the same actor twice – first when playing Orestes (in their initial encounter), then as Orestes' servant (who reports her brother's victory). See Luschnig (1995, 131 n.105).

33 Electra quotes Aegisthus earlier in the play (*El.* 330–31), perhaps providing the template for his 'sound'. De Jong (1991, 132–34, 153–54, 161–62) analyses the way the Messenger 'focalizes' his account, privileging one point of view over another.

34 They also learn of the shield of Achilles from a sailor in the port of Nauplion (*El.* 452–53), a detail picked up when Castor announces that Helen and Menelaus have just arrived at Nauplion (1278–79). In this way, Euripides subtly 'frames' the news of the beginning and the end of the Trojan War.

35 De Jong (2003, 382–88).

36 According to Henrichs (2000, 187), 'This is arguably the most graphic account of a homicide in the extant plays of Euripides'. For some, Aegisthus's death simply represents the tyrant's long-overdue punishment (Lloyd 1986, 15–16; Gellie 1981, 6). In Burnett's view (1998, 235), the word 'convulsions' (used for deaths in Homer) even adds a heroic dimension to Orestes' deed. However, Homeric deaths generally occur in battle, face to face, not at a sacrifice with a cleaver brought down on the victim's back. The garden-like setting, Aegisthus's hospitality as host, the sacrifice that

shifts from animal to human victim, and the visceral details raise serious doubts about the justice meted out by Orestes. See Verheij (2016, 769–77), Sourvinou-Inwood (2003, 346–47, 349), de Jong (2003, 384–88), Raeburn (2000, 160–62), Porter (1990, 255–60, 275–78), Easterling (1988, 101–7), and Arnott (1981, 181–83).

37 Foley (2001, 234–42) provides a useful comparison of the several tragic Clytemnestras.

38 The Latin name for Polydeuces is Pollux, which gives us the names for the prominent stars in the constellation Gemini, namely Castor and Pollux.

39 The temple to the twin-gods in Agrigento, Sicily, dating from the mid-fifth century BC, seems to have honoured the Dioskouroi, which could explain Castor's reference to returning to the sea around Sicily. In their role as protectors of sailors, the twins also appear *ex machina* at the end of Euripides' *Helen* (1495–1505, 1664).

40 'Castor and Pollux appear to make the best of a bad job' (England 1926, 104); Castor's 'aborted attempt to explain Apollo's purpose underlines the pointless nature of the matricide' (Dunn 1996, 139). See also Morwood (2002, 42–43), Hartigan (1991, 123–26), Whitman (1974, 133), Conacher (1967, 209–10), and McDermott (1984, 107), who sees only 'moral chaos' at the end of the play. However, some scholars think that Castor and Polydeuces present 'a more balanced understanding of the workings of Justice than is given to man in the entanglement of action and passion' (Zuntz 1955, 68), a view shared by Van Emde Boas (2017, 159–64) and Cropp (2013, 11–12; but cf. on 1238–91). Andújar (2016) emphasizes the irresolvable tension between the Dioskouroi's divine status and their familial concern for their mortal relatives.

41 Euripides' *Helen*, 1642–79. The version of the story in which a phantom Helen goes to Troy (rather than the woman herself) first appears in the early sixth-century BC *Palinode* by Stesichorus; his *Oresteia* is discussed in Chapter 3.

Chapter 5

1 Herington (1985, esp. 1–40) provides the classic account of the influence of earlier Greek poetry (much of it sung and accompanied) on the

development of tragedy. Wilson (2002, 39) takes the idea much further: 'Greek tragedy was a fundamentally musical experience . . . Tragedy was much closer to what we might term "choral opera" than "theatre"'. This view ignores the fact that roughly seventy per cent of the lines in extant tragedy are in dialogue metre, spoken without instrumental (*aulos*) accompaniment. As for tragic lyric, the sung/chanted poetry by the Chorus possesses a linguistic complexity much greater than opera libretti, which tend towards simplicity that allows the words to serve the music.

2 For imagery of gold in the play, see Maxwell-Stuart (1971). Seaford (2004, 153) rightly stresses the difference between gold as talisman (the golden lamb) or as an aspect of identity (Achilles' shield), and the use of gold as impersonal 'money'.

3 The engraved armour of Achilles resembles the shield of Phidias's ivory and gold statue of Athena Parthenos that stood in the Parthenon (Csapo 2009, 102–3), well known to the fifth-century Athenians. Csapo also notes that the adjective 'black' (*kelaina*, *El.* 477) modifying 'dust' is the normal Homeric epithet for 'blood'. The dust engraved on the sword evokes the (black) blood of Hector (named at 469) spilled on the ground when Achilles drags his corpse around Troy. These details add to the sense of waste that comes with Castor's revelation that the Trojan War was fought for a phantom.

4 This speech exemplifies *epeideixis*, oratory 'fit for display', one of Aristotle's three branches of rhetoric (*Art of Rhetoric* I.iii.1–3), which aims to convey praise (on ceremonial occasions) or blame (as here). Aristotle's *Rhetoric* includes seventeen quotations from Euripides, five from Sophocles, and none from Aeschylus. See Garland (2004, 19); also Scodel (1999–2000) and van Emde Boas (2017, 130–41).

5 A similar scene occurs in Sophocles' *Electra*, where Clytemnestra allows her daughter to speak (S. *El.* 556–57), but then silences her after she does so (626–29). Euripides' Electra demonstrates a keen interest in the structure of her 'free' response to her mother: 'Then I will speak, making this wish my preamble' (*prooimion*, 1060), the term used by orators for the formal opening of a public address (Roisman 2004, and Mossman 2001). On rhetoric in Euripides, see Conacher (1981 and 1998), Goldhill (1986a), and Gallagher (2003, esp. 406–12), who emphasizes the sophistic qualities of Electra's speech. For Sophistic influence in Euripides generally, see de Romilly (1992, *passim*).

6   Electra uses the same word (*charita*, 61) for Clytemnestra's 'gift' to
    Aegisthus, when she cast her daughter out of the house.

7   Denniston (1939, on 337) thinks that such repetition by Euripides 'often
    degenerates into a mannerism'. Roisman and Luschnig (2011, on 89) argue
    that Orestes uses verbal repetition to help mask his identity. On this
    tendency in Euripidean choral lyric, see Breitenbach (1934, 214–26).

8   Castor delivers some twelve imperatives; the play includes sixty-one
    others, as well as six self-exhortations and two second-person
    prohibitions (Roisman and Luschnig 2011, on 112–13). The god also
    refers to eighteen places by name, pointing to the diaspora that lies
    ahead, but also bookending the Farmer's prologue, with its plethora
    of place names (see Chapter 2, 'The Farmer'; also Roisman and Luschnig
    2011, on 1312–13).

9   Before her union with Aegisthus in Hades, Clytemnestra recounts another
    marriage to death – that of her daughter Iphigenia, sacrificed by
    Agamemnon at Aulis under the smokescreen of a wedding to Achilles (*El.*
    1020–29). Greek tragedy often treats this subject; see Rehm (1994) and
    Seaford (1986 and 1987).

10 Euripides deals with this story in *Iphigenia in Aulis*, beautifully presented
    in Michael Cacoyannis's film *Iphigenia*. We discuss Cacoyannis's *Electra*,
    the first film in his 'Trojan trilogy', in Chapter 9.

11 Nemea lies only twenty miles from Argos; Isthmia is thirty miles away.
    Orestes will pass through Isthmia (*El.* 1288) on his way to Athens.
    Olympia lies further west in the Peloponnese; Orestes tells Aegisthus he
    and Pylades are heading there for the games (781–82). Delphi is the site of
    Apollo's oracle, which Orestes visits (87) before the start of the play.

12 Miller (2004).

13 March (2014, 'Oenomaus', 'Pelops', with references); Pausanias, *Description
    of Greece*, 5.10.6, 6.21.9–11.

14 Discussed briefly in Chapter 3, the chariot race in Sophocles' *Electra* draws
    on this myth (S. *El.* 504–14); see Finglass (2007) and March (2001) on
    504–15. Euripides also refers to the story in *Orestes* (988–96, 1547–48) and
    Helen (386–87).

15 Kraus (1992) sees their assumed Thessalian identity as a reference to
    Achilles, the most famous hero from Thessaly. His armour provides the
    subject of the first *stasimon*, and Achilles may serve as a model (or foil) for
    Orestes.

16 Myrick (1994, 138–41, 148).

17 Roisman and Luschnig (2011, on 859–79) note that the Chorus reverse the standard epinician trope of comparing athletes *to* mythological characters. Pindar, the greatest of epinician poets, often includes the crowning of athletic victors (*Ol.* 9.84, 13.33; *Nem.* 4.88; *Is.* 2.16, 5.62, 8.64; etc.).

18 Seaford (1994), Foley (1985), Zeitlin (1965).

19 Cropp (2013, on 50–53) labels these 'conclusive reflections'. Paley (1872, vi–viii) and van Emde Boas (2017, 40–47, 132–34, 168–71) discuss 'gnomic' (proverbial) utterances in the play. On everyday speech in Euripides, see Aristophanes, *Frogs* 939–43; Aristotle, *Art of Rhetoric* III. 2.5; Paley (1872, x–xvi); and Collard (2018, 185–202, 207–13).

Chapter 6

1 Aristotle (*Poetics* 1449a 18) mentions scene painting, presumably on wood or canvas, removable from the wooden *skênê* building. This scenic element may have differentiated the settings between individual plays, although not as extensively as some scholars imagine. During the City Dionysia, the *skênê* building provided the backdrop for three different tragedies and a satyr play on each day of the tragic competitions, and for five comedies (each by a different playwright) on the day devoted to comedy. Given these constraints, language offered the most effective means by which the tragedians could create the visual world of their plays. Elaborately designed sets can lead contemporary audiences to find the verbal description in Greek tragedy redundant, or a sign of bad playwriting.

2 These distances are virtual, not real; to walk from the northern border of Argos (where Euripides locates the cottage) to the southern area where the Tanaus river cuts through Sparta and the Argolid (the old shepherd's dwelling) would take two full days. Both Sparta and Argos (an Athenian ally) claimed this southern border territory during the Peloponnesian War (Thucydides 5.41). Depending on the date of *Electra*, the reference to this area may have reminded the fifth-century audience of the battles fought between the Argives and Spartans around 417–16 BC (Roisman and Luschnig 2011, on 410–11).

3 The word 'foot/leg' (*poda*) occurs over twenty times in the play, and verbs for walking another eleven. In order to convey the physicality in the

language, the translations in this section sound purposefully awkward. In actable English, 'After we took our feet from this dwelling' might come out 'We left here with purpose', or 'When we made our way from the cottage'. Nevertheless, a good translation of *Electra* should convey the physical reality embedded in the ancient Greek language and experience, something we have lost in our own.

4 Cropp (2013, on 215–99, '*staging*') describes the almost humorous effect of this back-and-forth movement. During the 'chase', Electra calls on Apollo for help. Cropp assumes (on 216–21) that she refers to a small aniconic column dedicated to Apollo *aguieus* ('of the ways', protecting comings and goings) that some Greeks placed outside their homes. This seems unlikely for a poor farmer's cottage out in the country. Electra probably calls on Apollo as she might on any god, with the added significance that Castor later blames the lord of Delphi for the matricide.

5 The description recalls the famous epithet 'swift-footed' that Homer uses for Achilles, also suggested by Euripides (439 and 451). Given Orestes' reluctance to identify himself (even among friends), the evocation of the heroic Achilles seems ironic (Mulryne 1977, 36–37).

6 The Old Man hints at the labour involved in preparing what he brings: he has 'pulled the new-born lamb' from its mother, and taken the cheese 'from the cheese press' (*El.* 494–96).

7 Worman (2018, 194–98) examines 'sinister hands' in *Electra*. For tragic corporality generally, see Griffith (1998).

8 Euripides does something similar in *Hecuba* – the Trojan queen wishes that her hands, hair, arms, and feet could make her plea to Agamemnon more convincing, because words on their own have failed (Eur. *Hec.* 836–40).

9 These references to costume and appearance 'offer clues to characterization' (Wyles 2011, 51–52, 76–77). However, Kubo (1967, 23) errs in assuming that the Chorus are already dressed for the festival; they clearly state it will take place 'two days / from now' (*El.* 171–72), the Greek meaning for 'on the third day'. Costume played a key role in the Heraia festival itself, where Argive maidens presented a new robe to the goddess, possibly for her 'sacred marriage' to Zeus (Cropp 2013, on 165–212).

10 Electra may have learned this skill as a child (*El.* 539–42). For weaving and the recognition scene, see Torrance (2013, 16–19).

11 'Rags again!' comments Denniston (1939 on 501); also Muecke 1982. In *Acharnians*, Aristophanes mocks Euripides for costuming his characters this way (*Ach.* 410–17).

12 Earlier Electra describes these Asian slaves as wearing 'rich Trojan robes with golden brooches / to fasten them' (*El.* 317–18), useful information for a costume designer working on a production. Stieber (2009, 305, 314, 317–18, 329) looks at the visual contrast between luxury and poverty in the play.

13 We might compare this pathetic gesture to cover up their crime with that of Orestes in *Choephori*, who presents the evidence of Clytemnestra's guilt by laying out the net she used to trap Agamemnon in the bath (A. *Cho.* 980–1004). In Sophocles' *Electra*, the disguised Orestes displays a covered body, which Aegisthus thinks is that of the dead Orestes, until he pulls off the cover and sees Clytemnestra's corpse (S. *El.* 1466–80).

14 The Greeks also associated myrtle with death, fitting for the way Aegisthus's sacrifice will end. Electra says that her father's grave has no myrtle branches (Eur. *El.* 324); the Tutor remedies this when he visits Agamemnon's tomb (512).

15 It seems likely that the two men remain garlanded throughout the scene with Aegisthus's corpse. However, Orestes could offer his 'crown' to Apollo (Cropp 2013, on 890–92); or remove it on entering the cottage, acquiescing to the matricide (985–87); or throw it away after the murder ('Who would look on my head?', 1196), which Burnett (1998, 228 n.10) suggests. As for Aegisthus, would he still be wearing his myrtle garland when his corpse is brought on stage? Or did his violent death dislodge it? Euripides gives the director dramatically powerful choices.

16 Miller (2018, 39) argues that 'the spectral presence of the loser in the poetics of athletic victory' means that the 'poetry of victory is, simultaneously, the poetry of defeat'. If so, the 'spectral loser' in *Electra* lives up to that name, for he appears as a corpse.

17 Sheep take the stage to great comic effect in Euripides' satyr play *Cyclops*, lines 36–83.

18 Kubo (1967, 19–20). What happens to the Old Man's food and wine, and to Electra's jug of water? Perhaps she takes them inside when she goes to prepare a meal for the strangers (*El.* 425). Or the food could remain onstage, forgotten by the characters, but not by the audience, who see vestiges of 'normal life' that the play will soon leave behind.

19 Clytemnestra's entrance resembles her husband's arrival in Aeschylus's
   Agamemnon (*Ag.* 783–809); he also enters in a horse-drawn wagon,
   accompanied by *his* Trojan slave, Cassandra. For stage vehicles in *Electra*
   and other Greek tragedies, see Ley (2007, 70–83).

20 Offstage props proliferate in the Messenger's description of Aegisthus's
   sacrifice, and Euripides introduces a 'trail of possible murder weapons'
   (Arnott 1973, 56; also de Jong 1991, 161–62).

21 In Chapter 7, we unpack various meanings of *hubrizein*. Orestes and
   Electra's language recalls Achilles' violation of Hector's corpse in the *Iliad*,
   and Creon's refusal to bury Polyneices' body in Sophocles' *Antigone*. These
   actions exemplified moral error in the Greek world, where burial of the
   dead was sacrosanct. Sophocles' Electra also suggests that Orestes violate
   Aegisthus's corpse by denying it a proper burial (S. *El.* 1487–90).

22 Euripides mirrors the end of Aeschylus's *Choephori*, when Orestes reveals
   the corpses of his victims on the *ekkuklêma*. Unlike Aeschylus (and
   Sophocles), Euripides denies Aegisthus and Clytemnestra knowledge of
   the other's fate before they are killed.

23 These include von Schlegel (1815, 167), Paley (1874 on 894), Headlam
   (1901, 99), O'Brien (1964), Conacher (1967, 207), Sider (1977, 16–17),
   Mulryne (1977, 36–37), Tarkow (1981, 144–45), Halleran (1985, 15),
   Michelini (1987, 214–15), and Hammond (1984, 373–75), who contrasts
   Electra carrying her water jug with her holding Aegisthus's head.
   Denniston (1939, on 894–95) thinks that the killers bring Aegisthus's body
   along with his head impaled on a stake, like the Persian Mardonius who
   beheads Leonidas after Thermopylae (Hdt. 9.78.1–9.79.2). Those who
   reject decapitation point out that the Messenger says that Orestes brings
   back Aegisthus without specifying his *head* (Kovacs 1987; also Gellie 1981,
   11 n.12; Hartigan 1991, 118–19 n.29; Kraus 1992, 161; Marshall 1999–
   2000, 334; Raeburn 2000, 161–63; Roisman and Luschnig 2011, on 854–57;
   Cropp 2013, on 855–57).

24 A popular motif in Greek art, gorgons were depicted either as a free-
   floating face or head, usually with snakes for hair, or as a mask-like face
   appended to a body. See Phinney (1971).

25 Ogden (2008, 12–17).

26 In Euripides' *Andromeda* (produced in 412 along with *Helen*), Perseus
   carries the gorgon's head in his bag (Collard, Cropp, and Gibert 2004,
   fragments 137 and 142).

27 References to Perseus's story fit the context of the play, for the hero eventually founds the city of Mycenae, while maintaining close ties to Argos, Sparta, and Athens.

28 In Euripides' *Orestes*, Orestes taunts the Phrygian slave for 'being afraid of turning into stone, as if catching sight of the Gorgon'. The slave replies, 'No, I'm afraid of turning into a corpse; I've never heard of the Gorgon's head' (*Or.* 1520–21).

29 Later mythographers including Apollodorus (2.1.5) and Pausanias (2.24.2) report that the Danaids beheaded the Egyptian husbands they were forced to marry.

30 Foley (1980).

31 The specificity of Electra's language reflects the details of Perseus's story, where petrifaction would result from direct mutual eye contact with Medusa (Ogden 2008, 50–54).

32 Ancient audiences may have recognized a parody of the traditional ritual lament for the dead. For common elements, see Alexiou (2002, 161–84). In her monody, Electra laments 'continually, day by day' (145). She speaks similarly to Aegisthus's corpse: 'Every morning I never let up / rehearsing what I wanted to say to your face' (909–10).

33 The term *prosôpon* is the same word used for an actor's mask. The Chorus also refer to the 'pale face' (*leukon te prosôpon*, 730) and 'golden face' (*chrysôpon*, 740) of the sun; Orestes describes the sunrise as 'the white eye [face] of dawn' (*leukon omm'*, 102).

34 Several editors bracket lines 685–89, others bracket 688–92, suspecting interpolation or sensing an otherwise compromised text. Some substitute *hêpar* ('liver') for *kara* ('head', 688), the innards being the usual location for a suicidal blow in tragedy. If the lines are by Euripides, however, then *kara* – as the less conventional word-choice – is more likely; interpolators tend to avoid odd or unexpected diction.

Chapter 7

1 As well as the wordplay (*thêlu/thalos*), the term 'shoot' implies offspring, impossible for a married virgin like Electra (Roisman and Luschnig 2011, on 14–15). The Farmer fails to mention Agamemnon's third child,

Iphigenia, killed by her father at Aulis. Clytemnestra forcefully reminds us of her later (*El.* 1018–29).

2   As Burnett (1998, 243) points out, Aegisthus's marriage scheme for Electra constitutes 'a plot against her womb, an attempt to control what it might contain'.

3   In ancient Greece, 'marriage is for the girl what warfare is for the boy. For the young girl emerging from childhood it represents the normal goal of her sex, access to full femininity' (Vernant 1990, 99).

4   In her diatribe at Aegisthus, some think that Electra simply mouths accepted truisms about gender propriety (Van Emde Boas 2017, 129–41); others, that she strives for appropriate 'female speech' in a mixed company of men and women (Mossman 2001, 377–79). But for most readers of the play, what Electra says – and the strong possibility that she says it to the head of Aegisthus – makes this 'an intensely personal speech dominated by sexual insults . . . [showing] the obsessive nature of Electra's hatred' (Cropp 2013, 2; also Roisman and Luschnig 2011, on 914–51; Walton 2009, 146–47; Michelini 1987, 215–17; Arnott 1981, 183–84).

5   Clytemnestra levels the same charge against Helen's husband, Menelaus, a man with 'no idea how to control the wife who betrayed him' (*El.* 1028). Electra harangues Aegisthus for letting a woman rule the roost, yet she herself drives the action of the play: 'She implicitly subverts the gender hierarchy she explicitly endorses' (Hall 2010, 263).

6   Note the pointed redundancy of 'male father'. In Sophocles' version of the story, Electra taunts her sister Chrysothemis for this same failing: 'Instead of being called / the daughter of the noblest of all men, / you're known as the child of your mother' (S. *El.* 365–67). Passages like these provide further evidence that Sophocles and Euripides' plays were very much in dialogue.

7   Perhaps Euripides had the Chorus members (male performers wearing female masks and costumes) nod their assent.

8   Some adaptations of *Electra* (discussed in Chapter 9) develop the erotic Aegisthus-Electra attraction hinted at in Euripides' play.

9   Cropp (2013, 10–11, 24, and on 1139–46) and Foley (2001, 237) note similarities between Aeschylus's Clytemnestra and Euripides' Electra. Robinson Jeffers' *The Tower beyond Tragedy* and Eugene O'Neill's *Mourning Becomes Electra* (discussed in Chapter 9) develop this connection.

10 In Euripides' *Iphigenia in Aulis* (638–39), Clytemnestra says almost the same thing to her daughter Iphigenia: 'Of all our children, / you were always fondest of your father'.

11 The word Electra uses for 'arranging' the murder (*exartusomai*, 647) is the same the Farmer uses when he tells her to 'arrange things' in the cottage (*exartue*, 422). Euripides neatly captures the opposite poles of his Electra, both a mythic avenger and a farmer's wife.

12 Weiss (2018, 65–70) observes that Electra's commitment to lament sets her apart from the Chorus, even while she shares the lyric with them. The distinction disappears when the Messenger addresses the Chorus and Electra collectively as 'Mycenean maidens, glorious in victory' (*kallinikoi parthenoi Mukênides*, 761).

13 Tragedy incorporates elements of Doric Greek, which uses *êta* (*ê*) instead of the *alpha* (*a*) of the Ionic dialect, the vernacular of Euripides' Athens.

14 Carey (1995, 408–10) and Dover (1974, 207).

15 Electra later claims she is afraid to 'outrage' (*hubrizein*, *El*. 902) Aegisthus's corpse, and then proceeds to do so.

16 Castor uses the same construction to characterize the 'unholy wedding' (*anosiôn numpheumatôn*, 1261, i.e. 'rape') of Ares' daughter by Halirrhothius, prompting Ares to kill the perpetrator. The murder leads to the first homicide trial on the Athenian Areopagus.

17 In Aeschylus's *Choephori*, Orestes forces Clytemnestra into the palace so he can kill her by the side of Aegisthus: 'Sleep with him (*sugkatheud'*) in death, since you loved / that man, and hated the man you should have loved' (A. *Ch*. 906–7).

18 We learn later from Castor that Helen never actually went to Troy, so the myth of her infamous infidelity dissolves, making the deaths at Troy seem all the more meaningless.

19 Ancient audiences might have recalled the opening of Homer's *Iliad*, when Agamemnon quarrels with Achilles over another captured woman, Chryseis. Agamemnon says, 'I rank her higher than Clytemnestra, / my own wife – she's no way inferior / in looks, stature, mind, and what she can do' (H. *Il*. 1.113–15).

20 Most readers and scholars agree with March (1990, 63): 'In no way can he [Euripides] be called a misogynist'.

21 Larson (2001, 114–15, also 149–51).

22 Michelini (1987, 214); also Hall (2006, 77–80) and Kubo (1967, 28).

23 Leitao (2012, 52 –57) thinks that Euripides favours the 'single seed' idea of procreation championed by the sophist Anaxagoras, in which the father is the only real parent. This seems unlikely, given the emphasis in *Electra* on the role of mothers and the horror of matricide. Unaware that women produced the eggs that sperm impregnated, the Greeks thought that the male provided the seed for the embryo, and the woman the blood (because pregnant women stop menstruating, that blood must go to the unborn child). In spite of their biological confusion, most fifth-century Athenians would have recognized the truth of this passage from a lost tragedy of Euripides: 'A mother always loves her children more than a father: / she *knows* they are hers; he only *thinks* so' (Collard and Cropp 2008, fr. 1015).

24 Neither Aeschylus nor Sophocles mentions Agamemnon's ploy of a marriage to Achilles to lure Clytemnestra's daughter to her death, the subject of Euripides' *Iphigenia in Aulis*.

25 The shepherd describes the lamb as *neognon* ('newborn', 495); Clytemnestra uses the same word (*neognôn*, 1108) for Electra's purported 'offspring'.

26 In Sophocles' *Women of Trachis* (529–30), the Chorus use the image of a young animal torn from her dam to symbolize the trauma of a new bride separated from her mother (Rehm 1994, 74–75; Seaford 1986, 51–54). In Euripides' *Electra*, the lamb lost to her mother obviously suggests Iphigenia, but it might also apply to Electra.

27 *tekein* and its cognates also can refer to the father as 'begetter', a term Electra uses once for Agamemnon (*El.* 335). But the word occurs far more frequently in the context of a mother 'bringing forth' children: Clytemnestra, as 'bearer' of Aegisthus's children (62), and as 'birth-mother' of Orestes and Electra (116, 264, 640, 1061, 1212); Electra as potential 'bearer' of male offspring (22, 26), and who has (fictionally) 'given birth' (652, 653, 1127, 1129) to one. Sophocles uses the same word when Clytemnestra cries for mercy from Orestes: 'O child [one I bore], child [one I bore], / pity the one who bore you (*o teknon teknon, / oiktire tên tekousan*, S. *El.* 1410–11).

28 Euripides' Electra uses *mêtêr* ('mother') for Clytemnestra, but her Sophoclean counterpart never does so (Michelini 1987, 218 n.162). Sophocles downplays the importance of the matricide, saving the ultimate revenge for Aegisthus.

29 That very prospect motivated Aegisthus to marry Electra to the Farmer: 'He desired to weaken any children that I might bear' (*tekein m' eboulet' asthenê*, Eur. *El.* 267).

30 Cropp (2013, on 654) explains that the 'tenth-day sacrifice' following childbirth was designed to remove the 'defilement' of parturition from the mother. See Garland (1990, 94–98). Note that Kovacs (1998, n. p. 272) and Cropp (2013, on 1107–8) transpose lines 1107–8 to follow 1131; cf. Roisman and Luschnig (2011, on 1107–8).

31 As Hall (1993, 264) observes, 'It is difficult to appreciate the heroic justice of reciprocal blood letting when the victim thinks she has just become a grandmother'.

32 In Aeschylus, the gesture refers back to Clytemnestra's nightmare, in which she gives birth to a serpent that feeds at her breast, sucking blood with the milk (A. *Cho.* 523–51). In Euripides' *Phoenician Women*, Jocasta makes the same gesture (offstage, as in *Electra*) to try to persuade her sons to abandon their fratricidal combat (Eur. *Ph.* 1567–69). See generally Damet (2011).

33 Luschnig (1995, 120) points out that 'Orestes sees more of his mother than a son should'.

34 Goff (1991, 265).

35 Electra uses the same word *demas*, 'physical body', when she accuses Orestes of pitying Clytemnestra once he sees her arriving 'in the flesh' (*El.* 968).

36 Electra's clear disinterest in a normal marriage with Pylades undermines the claim (Zeitlin 2008, 323) that her 'newborn' plot arises from her deep longing to have children.

37 Orestes uses this expression earlier, having heard that his sister 'is yoked / in marriage' (*gamois / zeuchtheisan*, *El.* 98–99). See Seaford (1988, 135–36).

38 As the title of Walton (2009), *Euripides Our Contemporary*, suggests; over twenty years earlier, de Romilly (1986) entitled her study of the playwright *La modernité d'Euripide*.

Chapter 8

1 This change of setting provides the starting point for many interpretations of the play: 'Euripides' *Electra* administers some calculated shocks . . . by

setting the play on a poor farm outside Argos' (Vickers 1973, 588). For
Carey (2008, 99), the stage building as cottage 'shrinks the heroic world
and creates a more human scale for the action to follow'. Bernard (1985,
245–49) and Rivier (1975, 119–24) focus on the opposition of *chôra*
(country) and *polis* (city/palace) in *Electra*.

2 In his welcome to the strangers, the Farmer 'elevates' his ramshackle
home by calling the doorway 'gates' (*pulas*, 342 and 357). In tragedy,
this term usually refers to the double doors in the *skênê* building
representing the entrance to a palace (as in Aeschylus's *Choephori* and
Sophocles' *Electra*). The Old Man uses the same word, wondering what
will happen when Clytemnestra enters the 'gates' (*pulas*, 661) of the
cottage. Electra responds, 'From there it's but a short trip to Hades'
(662). Their exchange momentarily converts the Farmer's shack into a
palace-like setting, suitable for aristocratic bloodletting that consigns
the victim to the underworld.

3 Recall the Chorus's welcome to Clytemnestra: 'We honour you as equal to
a god, / blessed for your wealth (*ploutou*) and great good fortune' (994–
95). Ironies abound, for the Chorus know that this queen – far from
immortal, and far from fortunate – walks to her death in a smoke-
darkened cottage.

4 Ober (1989, 192–247, 'Class: Wealth, Resentment, and Gratitude'; 248–92,
'Status: Noble Birth and Aristocratic Behavior'); also Rosivach (1991) and
Denniston (1939, on 253).

5 Time and again, the play exposes the chasm between wealth and admirable
behaviour, demonstrating that noble birth does not equate to moral
superiority *vis-à-vis* the poor. See Carey (2008, 100–2), Gregory (1991,
123–24), Goldhill (1986, 161–65), and Jones (1962, 243–47).

6 As noted in Chapter 4, the actor returns in the roles of the Old Man, the
Messenger, and Castor. The last part allows for some ironic play with the
first, given that Castor instructs Pylades to take the Farmer with him and
provide him with 'abundant wealth' (*ploutou baros*, 1287). The audience
might remember the Farmer's earlier rejection of wealth *per se* as a
criterion for happiness (426–31); perhaps he would prefer to stay and work
his own land. Were there a sequel 2,400 years later, perhaps the good life in
Phocis would find the Farmer buying up farmland and orchards
for real-estate development, like Lopakhin in Chekhov's *The Cherry
Orchard*.

7 In their valuable commentary, Roisman and Luschnig (2011, on 137) make an uncharacteristic error, stating that 'the gods are not much on anyone's lips in this play'.

8 For the first view, Thury (1985, 21) claims that 'The Dioscuri soothe the troubled souls of Orestes, Electra and the chorus, providing each with virtue in their own terms'. Compare this interpretation with Michelini (1987, 226–27), who concludes that the gods oversee a 'pitiful triumph, representing not the saving of the house, but its collapse'.

9 As well as in *Heracles*, characters and Choruses accuse the gods of lacking wisdom and worse in Euripides' *Andromache* (*Andr.* 1029–36 and 1165–66), *Iphigenia among the Taurians* (*IT* 711–15), *Orestes* (*Or.* 28–31, 160–65, 191–94, 416–17, 590–95), and *Bacchae* (*Ba.* 1344–48). The dying Hippolytus wishes that humans could effectively curse the gods (*Hipp.* 1415). In *Suppliant Women*, Athena appears *ex machina* to restore a cycle of warfare that the play had struggled so hard to bring to an end (*Supp.* 1213–26). Unlike the case in *Electra,* no one on stage protests in *Suppliant Women*; Euripides leaves that to the audience.

10 For Lefkowitz (2016), Euripides' gods do not differ from those in Aeschylus and Sophocles. They are distant, unpredictable, cruel, but only seen from the limited perspective of humans. In her view, his plays do not mount a fundamental attack on their validity or credibility. For others, Euripides asks his audience why such gods should merit honour and respect (Lawrence 1998; Yunis 1988, esp. 169–71; Kerferd 1981, 163–72; Whitehorne 1978; Vickers 1973, 319–25; Kitto 1961, 209–10). According to Paley (1872, xxv), Euripides 'took delight in showing what a miserable set of deities men had formed for themselves out of their own imagination'. Verrall (1895, 96) concurs: 'Euripides presents interactions between man and the creatures of anthropomorphic fancy, saying the while to his audience, by all sorts of signs and whispers, "Such are the creatures which they would have us believe in, which they would make us adore. What kind of a figure do you think they make?"'

11 Electra echoes Orestes, who faults Apollo's 'obscure justice' that condemns him to banishment (*El.* 1190–93). As Pucci (2016, 90) concludes, 'Orestes unwillingly condemns the belief in the anthropomorphic theology, and weeps for himself as a victim of that belief'.

12 See https://www.theoi.com/Cult/ZeusTitles.html; also Cook (1914–40); and generally Gould (1985) and Versnel 2011 (esp. Chapter 2, 'Many Gods: Complications of Polytheism').

13 Cropp (2013, on 777–80) sees the place of Aegisthus's feast as a *locus amoenus* (Latin for 'pleasant place', literally 'place without duty or obligation'), which turns bloody. The same pattern occurs in the two lyric *stasima*, which begin in idyllic settings where the natural world seems at peace (flute-loving dolphins, the mountain glens of Pan) before swerving to Clytemnestra's murder at the end of each ode. This pattern continues until 'the countryside of Argos proves the scene of polluting murder' (Morwood 1981, 369).

14 Electra's change from 'ten suns' to 'ten moons' may point to Artemis (traditionally linked to the moon), the goddess who oversaw childbirth (Denniston 1939, on 1126).

15 Rehm (2002, 274–77); in Euripides' *Helen*, for example, Menelaus measures his long absence in terms of 'thousands of suns' (*Hel.* 652).

16 Hannah (2002, 21–25). However, his claim that the ancients associated the Hyades and Pleiades with bad weather is incorrect, for it depends on the season when the star clusters appear and disappear, as well as to whom – rain for the sailor in ancient Greece may bode trouble, but not for the farmer.

17 'Pleiad, n.' *OED Online*. Oxford University Press (December 2014. Web. 20 January 2015); Hesiod, *Works and Days* 618–23; and Theodossiou, Manimanis, Mantarakis, and Dimitrijevic (2011, on 'heliacal rising').

18 Rosivach (1978, 194–95) for Aegisthus; King (1980, 209) for Clytemnestra. King observes that Clytemnestra seems to grow out of the Gorgon, Sphinx, and Chimaera depicted on the armour, as if she were another female monster that requires a male hero to slay her.

19 Outside of Epirus and Thrace in the north, most rivers in Greece – including those mentioned here – were seasonal, dependent on rain and snowmelt. The appearance of the Hyades each year would signal their coming back to life.

20 Tammuz (2005, 155–56) clarifies the difference between open-water navigation in the ancient Mediterranean (basically unrestricted) and coastal navigation (extremely dangerous in the winter, December through February). The latter was important for those travelling by sea to the City

Dionysia, which began in the second week of March (modern calendar), when sailing close to land became less hazardous.

21 Recall that Electra addresses the sun, the earth, and the night sky as divinities (866–67), picking up her earlier lament to the night (54); see, generally, Cole (2004, 7–19).

22 Cropp (2013, on 727–36); cf. Rutherford (2007, 15) who notes Euripides' elliptical treatment of causality: 'Which side is Zeus on? . . . not inappropriate [to ask] in a play which so persistently explores moral uncertainties'. In an earlier version of the myth (ignored or suppressed by Euripides), the sun's about-face signalled that Atreus was the rightful ruler of Argos, forcing Thyestes to give up his stolen power. The Chorus invoke the same myth in Euripides' *Orestes* 1002–12 (Willink 1989, 253–58). Herodotus (2.142) describes the environmental effects of this celestial change. In Euripides' *Medea*, the Chorus imagine a more earthbound reversal of the natural order, with rivers flowing uphill to their sources, upending the traditional story that women are unfaithful, when men are the real culprits (Eur. *Med.* 410–30); compare Clytemnestra's comments on the masculine-driven double standard (Eur. *El.* 1030–40).

23 The Chorus seem to adopt Aeschylus's version in *Agamemnon* (in which Clytemnestra murders Agamemnon without the help of Aegisthus), supporting Electra's view that her mother was the agent in her father's death. As Grube (1941, 299) puts it, 'To Electra the murderer is Clytemnestra, with Aegisthus; to Orestes, it is Aegisthus, with Clytemnestra'.

24 Describing the effect of the first *stasimon*, Walsh (1977, 278) refers to Brecht's *Verfremdungseffekt* (discussed briefly in Chapter 4, note 26). Euripides employs the same technique in the second *stasimon*, when the Chorus pulls us into a mythic narrative only to step back from the story and view it critically.

25 Wright (2008, 127). Goldhill (1986, 256) also notes the 'uncertainty surrounding . . . the paradigmatic status of myth' in *Electra*.

26 Castor 'refute[s] the entire myth upon which the play has been based' (Hartigan 1991, 123). What the twin gods reveal about the Trojan War 'belatedly subverts the whole background of the story, just as other details of the play have subverted the plot-pattern of just revenge' (Mastronarde 2010, 185–86). Euripides drew on the *Palinode*, a lost poem by Stesichorus,

in which Zeus sends a 'phantom Helen' to Troy after transporting the real one to Egypt (Campbell 1991, 88–97; Finglass 2015, 93–96). In *Helen* (412 BC), Euripides fleshes out the story with surprising humour, but also with the suggestion of tragedy behind the apparent romantic-escape (Rehm 1994, 121–27). In *Orestes* (408 BC), Euripides reverts to the traditional story that Helen went to Troy, but the reasons for the war remain those put forward in *Electra*: Zeus wanted to decrease the human population and lighten the burden that mortals impose on the earth (Eur. *Or*. 1639–42).

27 Something similar occurs at the end of Euripides' *Andromache*, *Ion*, *Helen*, *Orestes*, and *Iphigenia in Aulis*, when a god or goddess tries to convert what looks like trouble into a happy ending.

28 *Frogs* 958. The second-century AD grammarian Athenaeus (561a) calls Euripides the 'philosopher of the stage'.

29 Burian (1997, 180). In a similar, but more cautious, vein, Scodel (1999–2000, 144) concludes that 'Euripidean theater could hardly fail to make its audience more aware of the dangers of being manipulated, more conscious of the need to distinguish a good performance from a worthy cause'.

30 Swinburne (1908, 36).

Chapter 9

1 From John Milton, Sonnet VIII (1642), in *The Complete Poems and Major Prose*, ed. M.H. Hughes, p. 140, New York: The Odyssey Press (1957).

2 Plutarch, *Life of Lysander*, 15.2–3. Another passage in Plutarch (*Life of Nicias*, 29.2–3) describes how much the Sicilians loved Euripides. The Athenian prisoners they had captured (following the Sicilian expedition in 413 BC) would recite speeches and sing choruses from his plays to gain extra provisions, and sometimes their freedom.

3 As well as the frequent productions at the major dramatic festivals, contemporary comic playwrights often refer to Euripides' tragedies, and the character 'Euripides' plays an important role in Aristophanes' *Acharnians* (425 BC), *Thesmophoriazusae* (414 BC), and *Frogs* (406 BC). As noted in Chapter 6, Aristophanes makes fun of the tragedian's fondness for rags, market-talk, democratic sentiments, clever (albeit suspect) rhetoric, tonal incongruities, and self-referential humour (Roselli 2005). A famous

fragment from the comic poet Cratinus coins the term 'Euripides-aristophantize' (*euripidarsitophanizôn*), pointing out the mutual interplay of the two (Kassel and Austin 1983, fragment 342). Euripides influenced the New Comedy of Menander as well, which features troubled engagements and marriages, mistaken identities, a surplus of recognition tokens, and domestic-flavoured dialogue. See Revermann (2016, 14–16 and 19) and Knox (1979); more broadly, Seidensticker (1982, 89–248).

4 Easterling (1997, 225); more generally, Revermann (2016). Dunn (2017) focuses on Euripides' popularity in the fourth century BC, noting the many references to his plays in Aristotle's *Poetics* and *Rhetoric*, in depictions on Attic and South-Italian vases, and in theatrical productions across the Greek-speaking world. Euripides' *Medea, Heracles, Trojan Women*, and *Phoenician Women* influenced the eponymous tragedies of the Roman Seneca (Lucius Annaeus Seneca, *c.* 4 BC–65 AD), as did *Hippolytus* for Seneca's *Phaedra*. We know of seven different Latin plays entitled *Electra*, but none are extant (Bates 1930, 91).

5 See Mastronarde (2017), on whom I have drawn extensively; also Cropp (2013, 33–36) and Garland (2004, 39–94).

6 Murray loved the theatre (his wife was a relative of W.S. Gilbert, of Gilbert and Sullivan fame); he wrote several (unsuccessful) plays; he was deeply involved in politics, helping to found the League of Nations and chairing its executive council after the Great War. Following the Second World War, he served as president of the United Nations Association, and was an early supporter of what later became Oxfam. See Stray (2007).

7 Macintosh (2016, 327–28).

8 As actor and director, Granville Barker's theatrical passions extended to many periods and styles. His play *The Voysey Inheritance* (1905) has had many successful revivals, and his *Prefaces to Shakespeare* (1927–46) remain a valuable guide to a theatrical understanding of Shakespeare's plays.

9 *Electra* was presented in repertory from January to March 1906, and January to February 1907, under Barker's direction. Gwendoline Bishop (also credited as Mrs. Clifford Bax) appeared in the Chorus. Three years later, as member of the People's Free Theatre for Poetic Drama, Mrs. Bax directed (and played the title role) in a new production of *Electra* at several locations in East London. Barker and Murray's Court Theatre productions clearly spawned new interest in staging Euripides' play.

10 Shaw (1907, Act. 3, Scene 2, 906–7, 913–14, 917–20, 932). Frequently called 'Euripides' during the play, Cusins earlier quotes a passage from Euripides' *Bacchae* (Act II, 871–80), using Murray's own translation.

11 A former student of Murray, and his successor as Regius Professor of Greek at Oxford, Dodds (1929, 97) describes Euripides and Shaw as 'philosophical dramatists'. Albert (2016) explores the many connections between the two playwrights, and between *Major Barbara* and Euripides' *Bacchae*.

12 MacCarthy (1907, 10).

13 Describing a passage of Murray's translation of *Medea*, T.S. Eliot (1928, 75) concludes that 'Professor Murray has simply interposed between Euripides and ourselves a barrier more impenetrable than the Greek language'.

14 Murray (1905, 3). For more accurate, and far more playable, English translations of *Electra*, see Introduction, note 1, or consult mine, freely accessed at this website: https://stanfordreptheater.com/electratranslation (see Figure 5).

15 From 1910 to 1962, at least eight different professional productions of Euripides' *Electra* used Murray's translation. The BBC broadcast Murray's translation as a radio play in 1929, 1948, and 1953, and ten university and schools mounted his translation of *Electra* in the United States and England between 1910 and 1955. See the Archive of Performances of Greek and Roman Drama (APGRD) http://www.apgrd.ox.ac.uk/.

16 Consult the APGRD website (previous note) for productions and adaptations of Euripides' *Electra* in England, Wales, Scotland, Cornwall, Ireland, France, Germany, Belgium, Holland, Poland, Spain, Italy, Iceland, Israel, Jordan, South Africa, Japan, New Zealand, Australia, the United States, Cyprus, and Greece. The most renowned Arabic translation is by Ismail El-Banhawi: Ministry of Information, Kuwait, 1974, in the World Theatre Series, Vol. 56 (روري بيديس, البانهوي, اسماعيل. 1974. من المسرح العالمي القديم من المسرح العالمي, 56. الكويت: وزارة العلام).

17 Born in 1942, Tsianos joined other natives of Larissa to found the Thessalian Theatre (*Thessaliko Theatro*) in 1975, and he directed many subsequent productions at Epidaurus. For more on his *Electra*, see http://www.apgrd.ox.ac.uk/productions/production/1105 (accessed 22 August 2019).

18 Rontiris directed Sophocles' *Electra* at Epidaurus that year, the performance taking place during the day because the theatre lacked electricity, a situation only corrected with the founding of the Epidaurus

Festival in 1955. The first modern staging of Euripides' *Electra* in that ancient theatre took place in 1969.

19 Koniordou (1953–) served as Greek Minister of Culture and Sports from 2016 to 2018. In an interview given on 16 March 2017, she addressed the importance of theatre today, and one senses that she was channelling Euripides: '[T]heatre is necessary today, more than ever. It was born in the 5th century B.C. to allow dialogue, freedom of thought and speech, conflict of ideas, acceptance of the other. These are basic values we need today desperately, because democracy can never be taken for granted. It is a living system that needs nourishing and protection from forces that may use tools of manipulation and fear to turn it into a new kind of tyranny or plutarchy (http://mag.politismosmuseum.org/koniordou/).

20 *New York Times*, review by Laura Cappelle, 2 May 2019. Played back to back with no intermission, *Électre/Oreste* opened in May 2019 in Paris and then travelled to the Epidaurus Festival in July. The trailer https://www.youtube.com/watch?v=JXAp6w6FiYg gives a good sense of the production in Paris. The graphic qualities had far less impact in the large outdoor theatre at Epidaurus. As the ancient Greeks knew, sound conveys descriptive immediacy far better than visual effects viewed from a great distance. In lieu of visual overkill, performances of *Electra* in ancient Greek (Wellesley College 1976, Cambridge University 1980–81, Kings College, London 1963 and 1993) tend to trust the words of the playwright to convey the essential dramatic experience.

21 Jeffers (1925).

22 Jeffers (1925, 62). We recognize elements from Euripides in the dirt and rags, and in the heroine's lost status. As Laks (1995, 125) puts it, 'Her filthy, ragged clothes represent the ugliness of her situation: a girl of such tender age, yet of such murderous hatred and able to dissemble with such finesse'.

23 Jeffers (1925, 65). Compare Euripides' Clytemnestra: 'I forgive you, daughter. Don't think / I'm all that happy with the things I've done. / How wretched have my own plans made me!' (*El.* 1105–6, 1109).

24 Jeffers (1925, 77–78).

25 Jeffers (1925, 81). The 'earlier fountain' appears to mean the world of nature, the 'first mother', uncorrupted by humans. This may represent Jeffers' transformation of the city in Arcadia that Castor tells Orestes he will found (Eur. *El.* 1273–75). Electra's solitary return to the house anticipates the ending of O'Neill's *Mourning Becomes Electra*, discussed below.

26 *New York Times*, 27 November 1950. *The Tower beyond Tragedy* ran for thirty-two performances. The public much preferred Jeffers' *Medea*, the greatest success of a play based on a Greek tragedy in the commercial theatre. As far as I can tell, Jeffers' Euripidean-inflected play has never been revived. In 1964, two years after Jeffers' death, Marian Seldes (the original Electra) recorded two sections of *The Tower beyond Tragedy*, including the powerful closing scene between Orestes and Electra (available on Folkways Records, FW 09767, FL 9767).

27 'Working Notes and Extracts from a Fragmentary Work Diary' (dated 'Spring 1926'), in Clark (1947) 530.

28 O'Neill (1931, 1053). Anyone familiar with O'Neill's tortured life will recognize autobiographical elements merging with his story of Electra. The playwright spent his career turning his personal demons into drama, and Greek tragedy proved a useful ally; see Sheaffer (1973).

29 O'Neill (1988a, 368; letter dated 28 August 1930). O'Neill had a long-standing interest in Euripides – he loosely based *The First Man* (1921) on *Medea*, and he drew on *Hippolytus* for *Desire Under the Elms* (1925). Although there is no direct evidence that he read Euripides' *Electra*, O'Neill spent six days 'studying Greek plays' as he prepared the second part of the trilogy (Black 2004, 171–72). His eldest son, Eugene O'Neill, Jr. (1910–50) became a classicist and taught at Yale, Princeton, and other universities, before committing suicide.

30 Freud and Jung reached back to Greek tragedy to name these concepts (Colman 2015, 'Oedipus complex', 'Electra complex'). Few today accept Jung's view that a girl's initial anger with her mother comes when she realizes she has been born without a penis. The same goes for Freud's belief that all young boys unconsciously wish to sleep with their mothers, and fear castration from their fathers. In *Mourning Becomes Electra*, these complexes are not – in psychoanalytic terms – complexes at all, for O'Neill's characters state their desires overtly, and more than once.

31 Giraudoux (1937). *Électre* opened at Théâtre de l'Athénée in Paris on 13 May 1937, directed by the great French actor and director Louis Jouvet (1887–1951), who frequently collaborated with Giraudoux.

32 Roisman and Luschnig (2011, 259–63) offer a useful summary of the many connections between the two plays. Moreau (1997) provides an excellent analysis of Giraudoux's play, from its roots in Euripides to its place in the pre-Second World War French theatrical scene.

33 Giraudoux (1964, 208). In Euripides' *Electra*, we only hear from Castor that
these spirits of vengeance will pursue Orestes to Athens (Eur. *El.* 1252–57,
1342–46).

34 'Électre, like her Euripidean counterpart, is dangerously unbalanced' (Laks
1995, 112).

35 In an interview in *Le Figaro* (11 May 1937), Giraudoux summarized his
approach to *Électre*: 'The thesis of my play is this: that humanity, by its
ability to forget, and by a fear of complications, absorbs great crimes
against it. But in every epoch surge forth these pure human beings who
don't want the crimes to be absorbed, and who prevent that absorption . . .
which only provokes more crimes and new disasters. Electra is one of
those beings. She attains her goal, but at the price of horrible catastrophes'
(Cohen 1968, 106).

36 In the United States when writing *Électre*, and unable to return to Europe,
Yourcenar oversaw an amateur production of the play in 1944 on Mount
Desert Island, Maine, where she was living. The professional premiere of
Électre, ou La chute des masques took place in Paris in 1954, and the play
was published the same year. Revivals have been staged in Quebec (2007),
and in Italian translation in Rome (1986 and 2017) and Turin (2002 and
2012). The analysis I present here draws extensively on Giove (2012).

37 Yourcenar (1971, 20), my translation. Yourcenar started Latin at 10, Greek
at 12, and her early interest in the Classics informed much of her later
work (Savigneau 1993, 50).

38 First quotation, Yourcenar (1984, Scene 4, p. 92); second, Yourcenar (1984,
Scene 1, p. 82).

39 Yourcenar honours the unity of place that French neoclassicists considered
an Aristotelian 'rule' for tragedy. Although Euripides does the same in
Electra (setting the action in front of the cottage), unity of place and time
does not apply to all Greek tragedies.

40 Yourcenar (1984, 109).

41 Yourcenar (1984, 113).

42 *Elektra*, 1962, was produced, directed, and adapted (from Euripides'
Electra) by Michael Cacoyannis; music by Mikis Theodorakis;
cinematography by Walter Lassally. For further analysis, see Bakogianni
(2011, 153–94) and Chiasson (2013).

References

Adams, S. M. (1935), 'Two Plays of Euripides', *Classical Review* 49: 118–22.

Aeschylus, *Oresteia* (*Agamemnon, Libation Bearers, Eumenides*), see Sommerstein (2008).

Albert, S. P. (2016), *Shaw, Plato, and Euripides: Classical Currents in* Major Barbara, Gainesville, FL: University Press of Florida.

Alexiou, M. (2002), *The Ritual Lament in Greek Tradition*, 2nd edition, revised by D. Yatromanolakis and P. Roilos, Lanham, MD: Rowman & Littlefield.

Andújar, R. (2016), 'Uncles *ex machina*: Familial Epiphany in Euripides' *Electra*', *Ramus* 45: 165–91.

Apollodorus, *The Library* (1921 [1996]), Vols. I and II, trans. J. G Frazer, Loeb Classical Library Nos. 121, 122, Cambridge, MA: Harvard University Press.

Aristophanes, *Acharnians* (1998), ed. and trans. J. Henderson, Loeb Classical Library No. 178, Cambridge, MA: Harvard University Press.

Aristophanes, *Thesmophoriazusae* (2000), ed. and trans. J. Henderson, Loeb Classical Library No. 179, Cambridge, MA: Harvard University Press.

Aristophanes, *Frogs* (2002), ed. and trans. J. Henderson, Loeb Classical Library No. 180, Cambridge, MA: Harvard University Press.

Aristotle, *Art of Rhetoric* (1926 [1991]), trans. J. H. Freese, Loeb Classical Library No. 193, Cambridge, MA: Harvard University Press.

Aristotle, *History of Animals* (1965), Vol. I, trans. A. L. Peck, Loeb Classical Library No. 437, Cambridge, MA: Harvard University Press.

Aristotle, *Poetics*, see Golden and Hardison (1981).

Arnott, G. (1973), 'Euripides and the Unexpected', *Greece & Rome* 20: 49–64.

Arnott, W. G. (1981), 'Double the Vision: A Reading of Euripides' *Electra*', *Greece & Rome* 28: 179–92.

Athenaeus, *The Deipnosophists* (*The Wise Banqueters*) (1937), Vol. VI, trans. C. B. Gulick, Loeb Classical Library No. 327, Cambridge, MA: Harvard University Press.

Bakogianni, A. (2011), *Electra: Ancient and Modern Aspects of the Reception of the Tragic Heroine* (Bulletin of the Institute of Classical Studies Supplement No. 113), London: Institute of Classical Studies.

Barrett, J. (2002), *Staged Narrative: Poetics and the Messenger in Greek Tragedy*, Berkeley, CA: University of California Press.

Bates, W. N. (1930), *Euripides, A Student of Human Nature*, Philadelphia, PA: University of Pennsylvania Press.

Beale, A., ed. (2008), *Euripides Talks*, London: Bristol Classical Press.

Bernard, A. (1985), *La carte du tragique: La géographie dans la tragédie grecque*, Paris: Editions du Centre National de la Recherche Scientifique.

Biles, Z. P. (2006–7), 'Aeschylus' Afterlife: Reperformance by Decree in 5th C. Athens?', *Illinois Classical Studies* 31/32: 206–42.

Black, S. A. (2004), '*Mourning Becomes Electra* as a Greek Tragedy', *The Eugene O'Neill Review* 26: 166–88.

Blaiklock, E. (1952), *The Male Characters of Euripides: A Study in Realism*, Wellington: New Zealand University Press.

Brecht, B. (2015), *Brecht on Theatre*, M. Silberman, S. Giles, and T. Kuhn (eds.), 3rd edition, London: Bloomsbury.

Breitenbach, W. (1934), *Untersuchungen zur Sprache der euripideischen Lyrik*, Stuttgart: Kohlhammer.

Burford, A. (1993), *Land and Labor in the Greek World*, Baltimore, MD: Johns Hopkins University Press.

Burian, P. (1997), 'Myth into Mythos: The Shaping of Tragic Plots', in P. E. Easterling (ed.), 178–208.

Burnett, A. P. (1998), *Revenge in Attic and Later Tragedy*, Berkeley, CA: University of California Press.

Campbell, D. A., ed. and trans. (1991), *Greek Lyric III*, Cambridge, MA: Harvard University Press.

Carey, C. (1995), 'Rape and Adultery in Athenian Law', *Classical Quarterly* 45: 408–17.

Carey, C. (2008), 'Country Matters: The Location of Euripides' *Electra*', in A. Beale (ed.), 94–102.

Chiasson, C. (2013), 'Re-politicizing Euripides: The Power of the Peasantry in Michael Cacoyannis' *Elektra* (1962)', in A. Bakogianni (ed.), *Dialogues with the Past* (Bulletin of the Institute of Classical Studies Supplement No. 126), 207–23, London: Institute of Classical Studies.

Clark, B. H. (1947), *European Theories of the Drama: With a Supplement on the American Drama*, revised edition, New York: Crown.

Cohen, R. (1968), *Giraudoux: Three Faces of Destiny*, Chicago, IL: University of Chicago Press.

Cole, S. G. (2004), *Landscapes, Gender, and Ritual Space: The Greek Experience*, Berkeley, CA: University of California Press.

Collard, C. (1975), 'Formal Debates in Euripides' Drama', *Greece & Rome* 22: 58–71.

Collard, C. (2018), *Colloquial Expressions in Greek Tragedy: Revised and enlarged edition of P.T. Stevens's* Colloquial Expressions in Euripides, Stuttgart: Franz Steiner Verlag.

Collard, C. and M. J. Cropp, eds. and trans. (2008), *Euripides, Fragments*, Vols. 7 and 8, Loeb Classical Library Nos. 504, 506, Harvard, MA: Harvard University Press.

Collard, C., M. J. Cropp, and J. Gibert, eds., trans. and comm. (2004), *Euripides, Selected Fragmentary Plays II*, Oxford: Oxbow Books.

Colman, A. M., ed. (2015), *Oxford Dictionary of Psychology*, 4th edition, Oxford: Oxford University Press.

Conacher, D. C. (1967), *Euripidean Drama: Myth, Theme and Structure*, Toronto: University of Toronto Press.

Conacher, D. C. (1981), 'Rhetoric and Relevance in Euripidean Drama', *American Journal of Philology* 102: 3–25.

Conacher, D. C. (1998), *Euripides and the Sophists*, London: Duckworth.

Cook, A. B. (1914–40), *Zeus: A Study in Ancient Religion*, 3 vols., Cambridge: Cambridge University Press.

Cousland, J. R. C. and J. R. Hume, eds. (2009), *The Play of Texts and Fragments: Essays in Honour of Martin Cropp*, Leiden: Brill.

Cropp, M. J. (1986), 'Heracles, Electra, and the *Odyssey*', in M. J. Cropp, E. Fantham, and S. Scully (eds.), *Greek Tragedy and its Legacy*, 187–99, Calgary: University of Calgary Press.

Cropp, M. J., ed., trans. and comm. (2013), *Euripides' Electra*, 2nd edition, Oxford: Oxbow Books.

Cropp, M. J., K. Lee, and D. Sansone, eds. (1999–2000), *Euripides and Tragic Theatre in the Late Fifth Century* (Illinois Classical Studies Vol. XXIV–XXV), Champaign, IL: University of Illinois Press.

Csapo, E. (1999), 'The *aulos* in Athens', in S. Goldhill and R. Osborne (eds.), *Performance Culture and Athenian Democracy*, 58–95, Cambridge: Cambridge University Press.

Csapo, E. (1999–2000), 'Later Euripidean Music', in M. Cropp, K. Lee, and D. Sansone (eds.), 399–426.

Csapo, E. (2002), 'Kallipides on the Floor-sweepings: The Limits of Realism in Classical Acting and Performance Styles', in P. E. Easterling and E. Hall (eds.), 127–47.

Csapo, E. (2003), 'The Dolphins of Dionysus', in E. Csapo and M. Miller (eds.), *Poetry, Theory, Praxis*, 69–98, Oxford: Oxbow Books.

Csapo, E. (2007), 'The Men Who Built the Theatres: *Theatropolai, Theatronai*, and *Arkhitektones*', in P. Wilson (ed.), *The Greek Theatre and Festivals: Documentary Studies*, 87–121, Oxford: Oxford University Press.

Csapo, E. (2009), 'New Music's Gallery of Images: The "Dithyrambic" First Stasimon of Euripides' *Electra*', in J. R C. Cousland and J. R. Hume (eds.), 95–109.

Csapo, E. and W. J. Slater (1995), *The Context of Ancient Drama*, Ann Arbor, MI: University of Michigan Press.

Damet, A. (2011), 'Le sein et le couteau: L'ambiguïté de l'amour maternel dans l'Athènes classique', *Clio: Femmes, Genre, Histoire* 34: 7–40.

Davidson, J. (1999–2000), 'Euripides, Homer and Sophocles', in M. J. Cropp, K. Lee, and D. Sansone (eds.), 117–28.

Davies, M. (1989), *The Epic Cycle*, London: Bristol Classical Press.

de Jong, I. F. (1991), *Narrative in Drama: The Art of the Euripidean Messenger-Speech* (*Mnemosyne* Supplement 116), Leiden: Brill.

de Jong, I. F. (2003), 'Three Off-stage Characters in Euripides', in J. Mossman (ed.), *Euripides: Oxford Readings in Classical Studies*, 369–89, Oxford: Oxford University Press.

Denniston, J. D., ed. and comm. (1939), *Euripides' Electra*, Oxford: Oxford University Press.

de Romilly, J. (1986), *La modernité d'Euripide*, Paris: Presses Universitaires de France.

de Romilly, J. (1992 [2002]), *The Great Sophists in Periclean Athens*, trans. J. Lloyd, Oxford: Oxford University Press.

Dickin, M. (2009), *A Vehicle for Performance: Acting the Messenger in Greek Tragedy*, Lanham, MD: University Press of America.

Dodds, E. R. (1929), 'Euripides the Irrationalist', *Classical Review* 43: 97–104.

Dover, K. J. (1974), *Greek Popular Morality in the Time of Plato and Aristotle*, Berkeley, CA: University of California Press.

Dunn, A. (2017), 'Euripides in the Fourth Century BCE', in L. K. McClure (ed.), 533–45.

Dunn, F. (1996), *Tragedy's End: Closure and Innovation in Euripidean Drama*, Oxford: Oxford University Press.

Easterling, P. E. (1988), 'Tragedy and Ritual: "*Cry 'Woe, woe', but let the good prevail*"', *Mètis* 3: 87–109.

Easterling, P. E., ed. (1997), *The Cambridge Companion to Greek Tragedy*, Cambridge: Cambridge University Press.

Easterling, P. E. and E. Hall, eds. (2002), *Greek and Roman Actors: Aspects of an Ancient Profession*, Cambridge: Cambridge University Press.

Eliot, T. S. (1928 [1960]), 'Euripides and Professor Murray', in *The Sacred Wood: Essays on Poetry and Criticism*, 2nd edition, 71–79, London: Methuen.

England, J. T. (1926), 'The *Electra* of Euripides', *Classical Review* 40: 97–104.

Euripides, *Electra*, see Kovacs (1998), Cropp (2013), and Roisman and Luschnig (2011).

Euripides (2008), *Fragments*, see C. Collard and M. Cropp (2008).

Finglass, P. J., ed., intro. and comm. (2007), *Sophocles' Electra*, Cambridge: Cambridge University Press.

Finglass, P. J. (2015), 'Stesichorus, Master of Narrative', in P. J. Finglass and A. Kelley (eds.), 83–97.

Finglass, P. J. and A. Kelly, eds. (2015), *Stesichorus in Context*, Cambridge: Cambridge University Press.

Foley, H. (1980), 'The Masque of Dionysus', *Transactions of the American Philological Association* 110: 107–33.

Foley, H. (1985), *Ritual Irony: Poetry and Sacrifice in Euripides*, Ithaca, NY: Cornell University Press.

Foley, H. (2001), *Female Acts in Greek Tragedy*, Princeton, NJ: Princeton University Press.

Foley, H. (2003), 'Choral Identity in Greek Tragedy', *Classical Philology* 98: 1–30.

Gallagher, K. (2003), 'Making the Stronger Argument the Weaker', *Classical Quarterly* 53: 401–15.

Garland, R. (1990), *The Greek Way of Life*, London: Duckworth.

Garland, R. (2004), *Surviving Greek Tragedy*, London: Duckworth.

Garvie, A. F, ed. and comm. (1988), *Aeschylus, Choephori*, Oxford: Oxford University Press.

Gellie, G. (1981), 'Tragedy and Euripides' *Electra*', *Bulletin of the Institute of Classical Studies* 28: 1–12.

Giove, M. (2012), 'Électre à Paris. J. Giraudoux, J.-P. Sartre, M. Yourcenar', *Revue italienne d'études françaises* 2, mis en ligne le 15 décembre 2012, consulté le 14 août 2019.

Giraudoux, J. (1937), *Électre, pièce en deux actes*, Paris: Bernard Grasset.

Giraudoux, J. (1964), *Electra*, in *Three Plays*, trans. P. La Farge and P. H. Judd, New York: Hill & Wang.

Goff, B. E. (1991), 'The Sign of the Fall: The Scars of Orestes and Odysseus', *Classical Antiquity* 10: 259–67.

Goff, B. E. (1999–2000), 'Try to Make it Real Compared to What? Euripides' *Electra* and the Play of Genres', in M. J. Cropp, K. Lee, and D. Sansone (eds.), 93–105.

Golden, L. and O. B. Hardison, trans. and comm. (1981), *Aristotle's Poetics: A Translation and Commentary for Students of Literature*, Tallahassee, FL: Florida State University Press.

Goldhill, S (1986), *Reading Greek Tragedy*, Cambridge: Cambridge University Press.

Goldhill, S. (1986a), 'Rhetoric and Relevance: *Electra* 367–400, *GRBS* 27: 157–71.

Goldhill, S. (1996), 'Collectivity and Otherness – The Authority of the Tragic Chorus', in M. Silk (ed.), 244–56.

Gould, J. (1985), 'On Making Sense of Greek Religion', in P. E. Easterling and J. V. Muir (eds.), *Greek Religion and Society*, 1–33, Cambridge: Cambridge University Press.

Gould, J. (1996), 'Tragedy and Collective Experience', in M. Silk (ed.), 217–43.

Gregory, J. (1991), *Euripides and the Instruction of the Athenians*, Ann Arbor, MI: University of Michigan Press.

Griffin, J. (2008), '"Hope Deferred Makes the Heart Sick": Euripides' *Electra*', in A. Beale (ed.), 103–9.

Griffith, R. D. (1998), 'Corporality in Ancient Greek Theatre', *Phoenix* 52: 230–56.

Grube, G. M. A. (1941), *The Drama of Euripides*, London: Methuen.

Hall, E. (1993), 'Political and Cosmic Turbulence in Euripides' *Orestes*', in A. H. Sommerstein, S. Halliwell, J. Henderson, and B. Zimmermann (eds.), *Tragedy, Comedy, and the Polis*, 263–85, Bari: Levante editori.

Hall, E. (2006), *The Theatrical Cast of Athens: Interactions between Ancient Greek Drama and Society*, Oxford: Oxford University Press.

Hall, E. (2010), *Greek Tragedy: Suffering Under the Sun*, Oxford: Oxford University Press.

Halleran, M. R. (1985), *The Stagecraft in Euripides*, London: Croom Helm.

Halporn, J. W. (1983), 'The Skeptical Electra', *Harvard Studies in Classical Philology* 87: 101–18.

Hammond, N. G. L. (1984), 'Spectacle and Parody in Euripides' *Electra*', *Greek, Roman, and Byzantine Studies* 25: 373–87.

Hannah, R. (2002), 'Imaging the Cosmos: Astronomical Ekprhaseis in Euripides', *Ramus* 31: 19–32.

Harder, M. A. (1995), '"Right" and "Wrong" in the *Electras*', *Hermathena* 159: 15–31.

Hartigan, K. V. (1991), *Ambiguity and Self-Deception: The Apollo and Artemis Plays of Euripides*, Frankfurt am Main: Peter Lang.

Headlam, W. (1901), 'Notes on Euripides, II', *Classical Review* 15: 98–108.

Henrichs, A. (2000), 'Drama and *dromena*: Bloodshed, Violence, and Sacrificial Metaphor in Euripides', *Harvard Studies in Classical Philology* 100: 173–88.

Herington, J. (1985), *Poetry into Drama: Early Tragedy and the Greek Poetic Tradition*, Berkeley, CA: University of California Press.

Herodotus, *The Persian Wars* (1938 [2000]), Vols. I–IV, ed. and trans. A. D. Godley, Loeb Classical Library Nos. 117–120, Cambridge, MA: Harvard University Press.

Hesiod, *Works and Days* (2018), in *Hesiod*, Vol. I, *Theogony, Works and Days. Testimonia*, ed. and trans. G. W. Most, Loeb Classical Library No. 57, Cambridge, MA: Harvard University Press.

Homer, *Iliad* (1924–25 [1999]), Vols. I. and II, trans. A. T. Murray, revised by W. F. Wyatt, 2nd revised edition, Loeb Classical Library Nos. 170, 171, Cambridge, MA: Harvard University Press.

Homer, *Odyssey* (1919 [1998]), Vols. I and II, trans. A. T. Murray, revised by G. E. Dimock, 2nd edition, Loeb Classical Library Nos. 104, 105, Cambridge, MA: Harvard University Press.

Jeffers, R. (1925), *The Tower beyond Tragedy*, in *Roan Stallion, Tamar, and Other Poems*, 29–82, New York: Boni & Liveright.

Jones, J. (1962 [1980]), *On Aristotle and Greek Tragedy*, Stanford, CA: Stanford University Press.

Kassel, R. and C. Austin, eds. (1983), *Poetae Comici Graeci*, Vol. IV, Berlin: Walter de Gruyter.

Kells, J. H. (1966), 'More Notes on Euripides' *Electra*', *Classical Quarterly* 15: 51–54.

Kennedy, A., trans. and adapt. (2001), *Electra (Euripides)*, in *The Adrienne Kennedy Reader*, 79–98, Minneapolis, MN: University of Minnesota Press.

Kerferd, G. G. (1981), *The Sophistic Movement*, Cambridge: Cambridge University Press.

King, K. C. (1980), 'The Force of Tradition: The Achilles Ode in Euripides' *Electra*', *Transactions of the American Philological Association* 110: 195–212.

Kitto, H. D. F. (1961 [2011]), *Greek Tragedy*, 3rd edition, London: Routledge.

Knox, B. (1979), 'Euripidean Comedy', in B. Knox, *Word and Action: Essays on the Ancient Theater*, 250–74, Baltimore, MD: Johns Hopkins University Press.

Kovacs, D. (1987), 'Where is Aegisthus' Head?', *Classical Philology* 37: 139–41.

Kovacs, D., ed. and trans. (1998), *Electra*, in *Euripides III: Suppliant Women, Electra, Heracles*, Loeb Classical Library No. 9, Cambridge, MA: Harvard University Press.

Kraus, C. S. (1992), 'Thessalian Orestes', *Materiali e discussioni per l'analisi dei testi classici* 29: 157–63.

Kubo, M. (1967), 'The Norm of Myth: Euripides' *Electra*', *Harvard Studies in Classical Philogogy* 71: 15–31.

Laks, B. C. (1995), *Electra: A Gender Sensitive Study*, Jefferson, NC: McFarland.

Lamari, A. A. (2017), *Reperforming Greek Tragedy: Theater, Politics, and Cultural Mobility in the Fifth and Fourth Centuries BC*, Berlin: Walter de Gruyter.

Larson, J. (2001), *Greek Nymphs: Myths, Cult, Lore*, Oxford: Oxford University Press.

Lawrence, S. E. (1998), 'The God That Is Truly God and the Universe of Euripides' *Heracles*', *Mnemosyne* 51: 129–46.

Lefkowitz, M. (2012), *The Lives of the Greek Poets*, 2nd edition, Baltimore, MD: Johns Hopkins University Press.

Lefkowitz, M. (2016), *Euripides and the Gods*, Oxford: Oxford University Press.

Leitao, D. D. (2012), *The Pregnant Male as Myth and Metaphor in Classical Greek Literature*, Cambridge: Cambridge University Press.

Lembke, J. and K. J Reckford, trans. (1994), *Euripides: Electra*, New York: Oxford University Press.

Ley, G. (2007), *The Theatricality of Greek Tragedy*, Chicago, IL: University of Chicago Press.

Lloyd, M. (1986), 'Realism and Character in Euripides' *Electra*', *Phoenix* 40: 1–19.

Lloyd, M. (1992), *The Agôn in Euripides*, Oxford: Clarendon Press.

Lloyd, M. (2005), *Sophocles: Electra*, London: Bloomsbury.

Lloyd-Jones, H., ed. and trans. (1994), *Sophocles*, Vol. I: *Ajax, Electra, Oedipus Tyrannus*, Loeb Classical Library No. 20, Cambridge, MA: Harvard University Press.

Luschnig, C. A. E. (1995), *The Gorgon's Severed Head: Studies of Alcestis, Electra, and Phoenissae, Mnemosyne* Supplement 153, Leiden: Brill.

MacCarthy, D. (1907 [1966]), *The Court Theatre 1904–7: A Commentary and Criticism*, ed. with additional material by S. Weintraub, Coral Gables, FL: University of Miami Press.

Macintosh, F. (2016), 'Conquering England: Ireland and Greek Tragedy', in B. Smit (ed.), 323–36.

March, J. R. (1987), *The Creative Poet: Studies on the Treatment of Myths in Greek Poetry, BICS* Supplement 49, London: Institute of Classical Studies.

March, J. R. (1990), 'Euripides the Misogynist?', in A. Powell (ed.), 32–75.

March, J. R., ed., trans. and comm. (2001), *Sophocles, Electra*, Warminster: Aris & Phillips.

March, J. R. (2014), *Dictionary of Classical Mythology*, 2nd edition, illustrations by N. Barrett, Oxford: Oxbow Books.

Marshall, C. W. (1999–2000), 'Theatrical Reference in Euripides' *Electra*', in M. J. Cropp, K. Lee, and D. Sansone (eds.), 325–41.

Marshall, C. W. (2017), *Aeschylus: Libation Bearers*, London: Bloomsbury.

Mastronarde, D. J. (1990), 'Actors on High: The Skene Roof, the Crane, and the Gods in Attic Drama', *Classical Antiquity* 9: 248–94.

Mastronarde, D. J. (1999–2000), 'Euripidean Tragedy and Genre: The Terminology and its Problems', in M. J. Cropp, K. Lee, and D. Sansone (eds.), 23–39.

Mastronarde, D. J. (2010), *The Art of Euripides: Dramatic Technique and Social Context*, Cambridge: Cambridge University Press.

Mastronarde, D. J. (2017), 'Text and Transmission', in L. K. McClure (ed.), 12–26.

Maxwell-Stuart, P. G. (1971), 'Gilden Euripides', *La Parola del Passato* 26: 5–13.

McClure, L. K. (2015), 'Tokens of Identity: Gender and Recognition in Greek Tragedy', *Illinois Classical Studies* 40: 219–36.

McClure, L. K., ed. (2017), *A Companion to Euripides*, Chichester: Wiley Blackwell.

McDermott, E. (1984), 'Euripides and the Decline of Character: A Soap Opera Connection', *Classical Outlook* (May/June): 105–8.

Michelini, A. N. (1987), *Euripides and the Tragic Tradition*, Madison, WI: University of Wisconsin Press.

Miller, P. J. (2018), 'In the Shadow of Praise: Epinician Losers and Epinician Poetics', *Bulletin of the Institute of Classical Studies* 61: 21–41.

Miller, S. G. (2004), *Ancient Greek Athletics*, New Haven, CT: Yale University Press.

Moreau, A. (1984), 'Naissance d'Électre', *Pallas* 31: 63–82.

Moreau, M.-C. (1997), *Électre ou L'intransigeance*, Toulouse: CRDP Midi-Pyrénées.

Moretti, J.-C. (1999–2000), 'The Theater of the Sanctuary of Dionysus Eleuthereus in Late Fifth-Century Athens', in M. Cropp, K. Lee, and D. Sansone (eds.), 377–98.

Morgan, E. S., trans. (1998), *Electra*, in D. R. Slavitt and P. Bovie (eds.), *Euripides 2*, Philadelphia, PA: University of Pennsylvania Press.

Morwood, J. (1981), 'The Pattern of Euripides' *Electra*', *American Journal of Philology* 102: 361–70.

Morwood, J., trans. (1997), *Euripides: Medea, Hippolytus, Electra, Helen*, Oxford: Clarendon Press.

Morwood, J. (2002), *The Plays of Euripides*, London: Bristol Classical Press.

Mossman, J. (2001), 'Women's Speech in Greek Tragedy: The Case of Clytemnestra and Electra in Euripides' *Electra*', *Classical Quarterly* 51: 374–84.

Muecke, F. (1982), '"I Know You – By Your Rags": Costume and Disguise in Fifth-Century Drama', *Antichthon* 16: 17–34.

Mulryne, J. R. (1977), 'Poetic Structures in the *Electra* of Euripides', *Liverpool Classical Monthly* 2: 31–38.

Murray, G., trans. (1905 [1923]), *Electra of Euripides,* London: George Allen & Unwin.

Myrick, L. D. (1994), 'The Way Up and Down: Trace Horse and Turning Imagery in the Orestes Plays', *Classical Journal* 89: 131–48.

Ober, J. (1989), *Mass and Elite in Democratic Athens: Rhetoric, Ideology, and the Power of the People*, Princeton, NJ: Princeton University Press.

O'Brien, M. J. (1964), 'Orestes and the Gorgon', *American Journal of Philology* 85: 13–39.

Ogden, D. (2008), *Perseus*, Abingdon: Routledge.

O'Neill, E. (1931 [1988]), *Mourning Becomes Electra*, in *Complete Plays 1920–1931*, Vol. 2, ed. T. Bogard, 866–1054, New York: Library of America.

O'Neill, E. (1988a), *Selected Letters*, ed. T. Bogard and J. R. Bryer, New Haven, CT: Yale University Press.

Paley, F. A., ed. (1872), *Euripides*, 2nd edition, Vol. 1, London: Whittaker.

Paley, F. A., ed. (1874), *Euripides*, 2nd edition, Vol. 2, London: Whittaker.

Papastamati-Von Moock, C. (2015), 'The Wooden Theatre of Dionysus Eleuthereus in Athens: Old Issues, New Research', in R. Frederiksen, E. R. Gebhard, and A. Sokolicek (eds.), *The Architecture of the Ancient Greek Theatre*, 39–79, Aarhus: Aarhus University Press.

Pausanias, *Description of Greece* (1918 [1961]), Vols. III and IV, ed. and trans. W. H. S. Jones, Loeb Classical Library Nos. 272, 297, Cambridge, MA: Harvard University Press.

Phinney, E., Jr. (1971), 'Perseus' Battle with the Gorgons', *Transactions of the American Philological Association* 102: 445–63.

Pindar (1997 [2012]), *Pindar*, Vol. I: *Olympian Odes. Pythian Odes*; Vol. II: *Nemean Odes. Isthmian Odes. Fragments*, ed. and trans. W. H Race, Loeb Classical Library Nos. 56, 485, Cambridge, MA: Harvard University Press.

Plutarch (1916 [1998]), *Lives*, Vols. III and IV, trans. B. Perrin, Loeb Classical Library Nos. 65, 80, Cambridge, MA: Harvard University Press.

Porter, J. R. (1990), 'Tiptoeing through the Corpses: Euripides' *Electra*, Apollonius, and the Bouphonia', *Greek, Roman, and Byzantine Studies* 31: 255–80.

Powell, A., ed. (1990), *Euripides, Women, and Sexuality*, London: Routledge.

Prag, A. J. N. W. (1985), *The Oresteia: Iconographic and Narrative Tradition*, Oxford: Oxford University Press.

Pucci, P. (2016), *Euripides' Revolution Under Cover: An Essay*, Ithaca, NY: Cornell University Press.

Raeburn, D. (2000), 'The Significance of Stage Properties in Euripides' *Electra*', *Greece & Rome* 47: 149–68.

Rehm, R. (1994), *Marriage to Death: The Conflation of Wedding and Funeral Rituals in Greek Tragedy*, Princeton, NJ: Princeton University Press.

Rehm, R. (2002), *The Play of Space: Spatial Transformation in Greek Tragedy*, Princeton, NJ: Princeton University Press.

Rehm, R. (2017), *Understanding Greek Tragic Theatre*, revised edition, London: Routledge.

Revermann, M. (2006), 'The Competence of Theatre Audiences in Fifth- and Fourth-Century Athens', *Journal of Hellenic Studies* 126: 99–124.

Revermann, M. (2016), 'The Reception of Greek Tragedy from 500 to 323 BC', in B. Smit (ed.), 13–28.

Ringer, M. (2016), *Euripides and the Boundaries of the Human*, Lanham, MD: Lexington Books.

Rivier, A. (1975), *Essai sur le tragique d'Euripide*, 2nd edition, Paris: de Boccard.

Roisman, H. A. (2004), 'Women's Free Speech in Greek Tragedy', in I. Sluiter and R. Rosen (eds.), *Free Speech in Classical Antiquity*, 91–114, Leiden: Brill.

Roisman, H. A. and C. A. E. Luschnig, eds. and comm. (2011), *Euripides'*
Electra: A Commentary, Norman, OK: University of Oklahoma Press.

Ronnet, G. (1975), 'L'ironie d'Euripide dans *Électre* (vers 513 a 546)', *Revue des*
Études Grecques 88: 63–70.

Roselli, D. (2005), 'Vegetable Hawking Mom and Fortunate Son: Euripides,
Tragic Style, and Reception', *Phoenix* 59: 1–49.

Rosivach, V. J. (1978), 'The "Golden Lamb" Ode in Euripides' *Electra*', *Classical*
Philology 73: 189–99.

Rosivach, V. J. (1991), 'Some Athenian Suppositions about the "Poor"', *Greece &*
Rome 38: 189–98.

Rutherford, R. (2007), '"Why should I mention Io?" Aspects of Choral
Narration in Greek Tragedy', *Proceedings of the Cambridge Philological*
Society 53: 1–39.

Savigneau, J. (1993), *Marguerite Yourcenar: Inventing a Life*, trans. J. E. Howard,
Chicago, IL: University of Chicago Press.

Scodel, R. (2017), 'The Euripidean Biography', in L. K. McClure (ed.), 27–41.

Scodel, R. (1999–2000), 'Verbal Performance and Euripidean Rhetoric', in
M. J. Cropp, K. Lee, and D. Sansone (eds.), 129–44.

Seaford, R. (1986), 'Wedding Ritual and Textual Criticism in Sophocles'
Women of Trachis', *Hermes* 114: 50–59.

Seaford, R. (1987), 'The Tragic Wedding', *Journal of Hellenic Studies* 107:
106–30.

Seaford, R. (1988), 'The Eleventh Ode of Bacchylides', *Journal of Hellenic*
Studies 108: 118–36.

Seaford, R. (1994), *Reciprocity and Ritual: Homer and Tragedy in the*
Developing City-State, Oxford: Clarendon Press.

Seaford, R. (2004), *Money and the Early Greek Mind: Homer, Philosophy,*
Tragedy, Cambridge: Cambridge University Press.

Segal, C. P. (1985), 'Tragedy, Corporality, and the Texture of Language:
Matricide in the Three Electra Plays', *The Classical World* 79: 7–23.

Seidensticker, B. (1982), *Palintonos Harmonia: Studien zu komischen*
Elementen in der griechischen Tragödie (*Hypomnemeta* v. 72), Göttingen:
Vandenhoeck & Ruprecht.

Shaw, B. (1907 [2008]), *Major Barbara, Definitive Text*, ed. N. Grene, London:
Methuen.

Shaw, F. (2010), 'Foreword', in L. Pilkington, *Theatre & Ireland*, ix–xii,
London: Palgrave Macmillan.

Sheaffer, L. (1973), *O'Neill: Son and Artist*, Boston, MA: Little, Brown.

Sheppard, J. T. (1918), 'The *Electra* of Euripides', *Classical Review* 32: 137–41.

Sider, D. (1977), 'Two Stage Directions for Euripides', *American Journal of Philology* 98: 16–19.

Sifakis, G. (2002), 'Looking for the Actor's Art in Aristotle', in P. E. Easterling and E. Hall (eds.), 148–64.

Silk, M. S, ed. (1996), *Tragedy and the Tragic*, Oxford: Clarendon Press.

Smit, Betine van Zyl, ed. (2016), *A Handbook to the Reception of Greek Drama*, Chichester: Wiley.

Sommerstein, A. H., ed. and trans. (2008), *Aeschylus II, Oresteia*, Loeb Classical Library No. 146, Cambridge, MA: Harvard University Press.

Sophocles, *Electra* (see Lloyd-Jones 1994).

Sourvinou-Inwood, C. (2003), *Tragedy and Athenian Religion*, Lanham, MD: Lexington Books.

Stieber, M. (2009), 'Coins and Character in Euripides', in J. R. C. Cousland and J. R. Hume (eds.), 255–72.

Stray, C., ed. (2007), *Gilbert Murray Reassessed: Hellenism, Theatre, and International Politics*, Oxford: Oxford University Press.

Swift, L. A. (2015), 'Stesichorus on Stage', in P. J. Finglass and A. Kelly (eds.), 125–44.

Swinburne, A. G. (1908), *The Age of Shakespeare*, London: Chatto & Windus.

Tammuz, O. (2005), '*Mare clausum*? Sailing Seasons in the Mediterranean in Early Antiquity', *Mediterranean Historical Review* 20: 145–62.

Tarkow, T. A. (1981), 'The Scar of Orestes: Observations on a Euripidean Innovation', *Rheinisches Museum für Philologie* 124: 143–53.

Theodossiou, E., V. N. Manimanis, P. Mantarakis, and M. S. Dimitrijevic (2011), 'Astronomy and Constellations in the *Iliad* and *Odyssey*', *Journal of Astronomical History and Heritage* 14: 22–30.

Thucydides, *History of the Peloponnesian War* (1928–35), Vols. I–IV, trans. C. F. Smith, revised, Loeb Classical Library Nos. 108–110, 169, Cambridge, MA: Harvard University Press.

Thury, E. M. (1985), 'Euripides' *Electra*: An Analysis Through Character Development', *Rheinisches Museum für Philologie* 128: 5–22.

Torrance, I. (2011), 'In the Footprints of Aeschylus: Recognition, Allusion, and Metapoetics in Euripides', *American Journal of Philology* 132: 177–204.

Torrance, I. (2013), *Metapoetry in Euripides*, Oxford: Oxford University Press.

Van Emde Boas, E. (2017), *Language and Character in Euripides' Electra*, Oxford: Oxford University Press.

Vellacott, P., trans. (1963), *Electra*, in *Euripides: Medea and Other Plays*, London: Penguin Classics.

Verheij, M. J. O. (2016), 'Hospitality & Homicide: Violation of *xenia* in Euripides' *Electra*', *Mnemosyne* 69: 760–84.

Vermeule, E., trans. (1959 [2013]), *Electra*, in *Euripides II*, ed. and trans. M. Griffith, G. W. Most, D. Grene, and R. Lattimore, Chicago, IL: University of Chicago Press.

Vernant, J.-P. (1972), 'Greek Tragedy: Problems of Interpretation', in R. Macksey and E. Donato (eds.), *The Structuralist Controversy*, 273–95, Baltimore, MD: Johns Hopkins University Press.

Vernant, J.-P. (1990), 'Oedipus Without the Complex', in J. P. Vernant and P. Vidal-Naquet (eds.), *Myth and Tragedy in Ancient Greece*, trans. J. Lloyd, 85–111, New York: Zone Books.

Verrall, A. W. (1895 [1967]), *Euripides the Rationalist: A Study in the History of Art and Religion*, New York: Russell & Russell.

Versnel, H. S. (2011), *Coping with the Gods: Wayward Readings in Greek Theology*, Leiden: Brill.

Vickers, B. (1973), *Towards Greek Tragedy: Drama, Myth, Society*, London: Longman.

von Schlegel, A. W. (1815), *A Course of Lectures on Dramatic Art and Literature*, Vol. 1, trans. J. Black, London: Baldwin, Cradock, & Joy.

Walsh, G. B. (1977), 'The First Stasimon of Euripides' *Electra*', *Yale Classical Studies* 25: 277–89.

Walton, J. M. (2009), *Euripides Our Contemporary*, London: Methuen Drama.

Weiss, N. (2018), *The Music of Tragedy: Performance and Imagination in Euripidean Theater*, Oakland, CA: University of California Press.

West, M. L. (1987), *Introduction to Greek Metre*, Oxford: Clarendon Press.

West, M. L. (1992), *Ancient Greek Music*, Oxford: Clarendon Press.

Whitehorne, J. E. G. (1978), 'The Ending of Euripides' *Electra*', *Revue belge de philologie et d'histoire* 46: 5–14.

Whitman, C. H. (1974), *Euripides and the Full Circle of Myth*, Cambridge, MA: Harvard University Press.

Willink, C. W., ed. and comm. (1989), *Euripides, Orestes*, Oxford: Clarendon Press.

Wilson, P. (2000), *The Athenian Institution of the* Khoregia: *The Chorus, the City, and the Stage*, Cambridge: Cambridge University Press.

Wilson, P. (2002), 'The Musicians among the Actors', in P. E. Easterling and E. Hall (eds.), 39–68.

Winnington-Ingram, R. P. (1969), 'Euripides, *Poiêtês sophos*', *Arethusa* 2: 127–42.

Wohl, V. (2015), *Euripides and the Politics of Form*, Princeton, NJ: Princeton University Press.

Worman, N. (2018), 'Electra, Orestes, and the Sibling Hand', in M. Telò and M. Mueller (eds.), *The Materialities of Greek Tragedy: Objects and Affect in Aeschylus, Sophocles, and Euripides*, 185–202, London: Bloomsbury Academic.

Wright, M. (2008), *Euripides: Orestes*, London: Bloomsbury.

Wyles, R. (2011), *Costume in Greek Tragedy*, London: Bristol Classical Press.

Yourcenar, M. (1971), *Électre ou La chute des masques*, in *Théâtre II*, Paris: Gallimard.

Yourcenar, M. (1984), *Electra or the Fall of the Masks*, in *Plays*, trans. D. Katz in collaboration with the author, New York: Performing Arts Journal Publications.

Yunis, H. (1988), *A New Creed: Fundamental Religious Beliefs in the Athenian Polis and Euripidean Drama* (*Hypomnemata* Vol. 91), Göttingen: Vandenhoeck & Ruprecht.

Zeitlin, F. I. (1965), 'The Motif of the Corrupted Sacrifice in the *Oresteia*', *Transactions of the American Philological Association* 96: 463–508.

Zeitlin, F. I. (1970), 'The Argive Festival of Hera and Euripides' *Electra*', *Transactions of the American Philological Association* 101: 645–69.

Zeitlin, F. I. (2008), 'Intimate Relations: Children, Childbearing, and Parentage on the Euripidean Stage', in M. Reverman and P. Wilson (eds.), *Performance, Iconography, Reception: Studies in Honour of Oliver Taplin*, 318–32, Oxford: Oxford University Press.

Zeitlin, F. I. (2012), 'A Study in Form: Recognition Scenes in the Three Electra Plays', *Lexis* 30: 361–78.

Zuntz, G. (1955), *The Political Plays of Euripides*, Manchester: Manchester University Press.

Index

Achilles 10, 13, 28, 71, 97, 134 n.11,
144 n.9, 144 n.15, 146 n.5,
148 n.21, 151 n.19, 152 n.24.
See also under Electra
(Euripides), Chorus, 'armour
of Achilles'
Aegisthus
before Aeschylus 33–34
in Aeschylus's *Oresteia* 12, 35, 40,
61, 157 n.23
in Euripides' *Electra*: banquet and
murder 13, 14, 15, 25, 26–27,
38–39, 41, 59–60, 72–73, 82,
84–85, 141–42 n.36; burial 32;
mistreatment of Electra and
Orestes 19, 21, 30, 34, 36, 37,
47, 48. *See also* decapitation;
see also under Electra,
'diatribe'; *see also under Electra*
(Euripides), 'corpses'
in Sophocles' *Electra* 37, 42–43, 96,
147 n.13, 148 n.21, 152 n.28
Aeschylus (523–454 BC) 11, 86, 112,
115, 122, 124, 143 n.4; *see also
individual characters by name*
Agamemnon: Agamemnon's
homecoming and murder
34–35, 38–39, 127, 148 n.19,
157 n.23; included in
Cacoyannis's *Elektra* 127;
influence on Jeffers 120;
sacrificial imagery 34, 39, 98
Choephori: Apollo 35, 40, 106;
corpses on *ekkuklêma* 35,
130 n.5, 147 n.13, 148 n.22;
kommos 53; matricide 35, 40,
43, 54, 99, 153 n.32; opening
scene at Agamemnon's tomb
35; recognition scene 36,
134 n.12, 136 n.7, 136 n.9;

scene shifts to palace 35, 38,
151 n.17, 154 n.2
Eumenides: Apollo 35, 87, 106;
Chorus departure from
orchêstra, 131 n.14; Orestes'
trial and ending 37, 40–42,
137 n.15
Oresteia trilogy 12, 34–36,
42, 135 n.5; *see also above,
individual play titles*
Suppliant Women 87
Agamemnon (*see also* Cassandra; *see
also* Iphigenia)
in Aeschylus, *see under* Aeschylus,
'*Agamemnon*'
in Euripides' *Electra*: murder 18,
19–20, 23, 28–30, 37, 39, 56, 61,
75, 105; raised by Old Man 8,
21, 24, 28; tomb 21, 24, 36, 41,
49, 66, 75, 107, 147 n.14
in Giraudoux's *Électre* 126
in Homer 13, 33, 135 n.3, 151 n.19
in post-Homeric poetry 34
in Sophocles' *Electra* 13, 61
Apollo: called on for help, 104,
146 n.4; oracle at Delphi
19, 144 n.11; prophecy on
matricide 28, 31, 40, 52–53,
61, 62, 105–06, 111, 139 n.16,
142 n.40, 155 n.11. *See also
under* Aeschylus, '*Choephori*',
'*Eumenides*'
Aphrodite 34, 94, 104
Aristophanes (446–386 BC) 6, 84,
115; *Acharnians* 135 n.5,
147 n.11, 158 n.3; *Frogs* 12,
112, 135 n.5, 145 n.19, 158 n.3;
Thesmophoriazusae 158 n.3
Aristotle (384–322 BC): *History of
Animals* 141 n.28; *Poetics* 17,

www.ingramcontent.com/pod-product-compliance
Lightning Source LLC
Chambersburg PA
CBHW070846030726
47504CB00005B/1235